GREEK COOKING

© ADAM EDITIONS-PERGAMOS S.A., KATSIMICHA, 190 02 PEANIA-ATTICA
TEL: 210 6644514-5, FAX: 210 6644512, e-mail.: pergamos@adam-editions.gr

302 TRADITIONAL RECIPES

GREEK COOKING

ADAM EDITIONS

In choosing recipes, we have endeavoured to select those which are the most representative of the Greek cuisine, which is why we have included many seafood dishes and recipes with pulses – among the favourites of the Greek family table – as well as a variety of delicious pies – specialities of various parts of Greece – soups, pasta and vegetable dishes, meat dishes and, of course, sweets and desserts. The traditional recipes offered here come from all over Greece and, apart from their variety and quality, they are also simple to make and have already been tried and tested by us. Precise and detailed instructions are complemented by attractive pictures to make your cooking session easy and enjoyable.

Our hope is that through the pages of this book, we will be able to transmit not only the recipes themselves, but also some of the tastes and scents of the dishes, which, cooked in pure olive oil and flavoured with the aromatic herbs – oregano, mint, thyme, dill, fennel and many other – growing abundantly on even the most arid-looking soil, adorn both the everyday and the festive Greek table.

Appetizers

Salads

Pites

Soups

Pasta

Sauces

Eggs

Vegetables

Poultry

Game   p. 164

Sweets   p. 172

appetizers

- Steamed mussels with wine
- Crayfish with oil and lemon
- Baked shrimps with cheese

Steamed mussels with wine
(Mydia achnista me krasi)

4 servings

1/2 kg mussels

1/2 teacup water

1/2 teacup white wine

White pepper, salt

Oil

Parsley

Place the water in a wide pan on high heat. When the water comes to a boil, put the mussels in, cover and boil for 8-10 minutes. Care is required so that they do not stick. Before removing from heat, add the wine, salt and pepper. Serve on platter garnished with parsley.

Crayfish with oil and lemon
(Karavides ladolemono)

4 servings

1/2 kg crayfish

1/2 teacup olive oil

Juice of 2 lemons

Vinegar, salt, pepper

Wash crayfish well and put into boiling water to which two tbsps of vinegar and 1/2 tsp salt have been added. Boil for half an hour and then clean. Serve with oil and lemon or mayonnaise.

Baked shrimps with cheese
(Garides saganaki)

6 servings

1 kg large shrimps

300 gr feta cheese

2 teacups olive oil

1 large tin peeled tomatoes

1 large onion, finely chopped

3-4 sprigs parsley

Oregano, salt, pepper

Boil the shrimps in a little water. Drain and reserve liquid. Sauté onion, add tomatoes, shrimp liquid, salt, pepper and boil until the sauce is thick. Arrange the shrimps in a clay or Pyrex baker and pour over sauce. Add finely chopped parsley, oregano and diced feta cheese. Bake in hot oven for half an hour.

Fried shrimps (Garides tiganites)

4 servings

1/2 kg shrimps, cleaned

1 teacup flour

1 cup milk

1 egg

1 tbsp oil

Curry powder

Salt, pepper

Oil for frying

Wash the shrimps well. Make batter in a bowl with flour, milk, egg, 1 tbsp oil, salt, pepper and curry power and mix well until the batter is smooth. Heat oil in a large frying pan; dip the shrimps one by one in the batter and fry until golden brown.

Savoury aubergine pasties

(Bourekakia apo melitzanes)

20-25 pasties

2 large black aubergines

Oil for frying

1 cup various grated cheeses

Rusk or toast crumbs

3 eggs

Flour

Salt, pepper

C lean the aubergines. Cut into thin slices. Flour and fry in hot oil. In a bowl put the grated cheeses, 1 egg, flour and a little pepper and mix well. Place a teaspoonful of the mixture on each slice of aubergine and fold up in a fat sausage shape. Beat two eggs with a little salt. Dip each pasty one by one in the egg first and then in the crumbs. Fry in hot oil.

Tomatoes stuffed with ham

(Domates yemistes me zambon)

6 servings

6 medium tomatoes

8 slices ham

6 tbsps mayonnaise

2 hardboiled eggs

Sugar

Salt

W ash tomatoes and cut a thin slice off tops. Hollow out tomatoes with a spoon. Put a little salt and sugar in each one. Chop ham, place in a bowl with the mayonnaise and mix well. Spoon filling into tomatoes. Peel the eggs, cut into 6 slices and put one slice on each tomato.

Tomatoes stuffed with ham
and cheese (Domates yemistes me zambon ke tiri)

8 servings

8 medium tomatoes

4 slices ham

4 slices graviera cheese

4 tbsps mayonnaise

4 pickled cucumbers

3 tsps capers

2 hardboiled eggs

Small lettuce leaves

W ash tomatoes, cut a thin slice off top and hollow out with a spoon. Chop the ham, graviera and pickles, place in bowl with the capers and mayonnaise and mix well. Stuff the tomatoes with this filling. Slice eggs and place one slice on each tomato. Refrigerate for an hour or so. Serve chilled on lettuce leaves.

4 servings

1/2 kg country-style sausages

1 teacup oil

1 teacup white wine

2 onions

Thyme

1 green pepper

Few drops lemon juice

Sausages cooked in wine
(Loukanika krasata)

W ash the sausages and cut into large pieces. Heat oil and sauté the onion until golden. Add the sausages and green pepper and stir well for a few minutes. Then add wine, salt, pepper, thyme and lemon juice. Simmer until done, adding water if necessary.

6 servings

1/2 kg onions

2 teacups olive oil

200 gr rice

1/2 kg vineleaves

Salt, pepper

Dill, parsley, mint

Lemon juice

Stuffed vineleaves (without meat)
(Dolmades yalantzi)

B lanch and drain vineleaves. Peel and chop onions; sauté in half the oil until golden. Add rice, salt, pepper, dill, parsley and mint (finely chopped), and half a glass of water. Cook until water is absorbed. On the dull side of each leaf, place a teaspoonful of the rice mixture in the middle and fold to make a little parcel. Continue until all filling and leaves are used up. Place dolmades, closely packed with smooth side up, in a large saucepan. Put a plate on top of them to keep them from opening. Add remaining oil, 2 cups boiling water and the lemon juice. Cover and cook over low heat. Serve cold, garnishing with lemon slices or hot, with egg and lemon sauce.

6 servings

1/2 kg dried butter beans

1 teacup oil

2 large onions

3-4 garlic cloves

3 red tomatoes or 1 tin peeled

  tomatoes

1 green pepper

1/2 teacup chopped parsley

2-3 bayleaves

Salt, pepper

Baked butter beans in tomato sauce
(Gigantes plaki)

S oak beans overnight in water. Boil until almost tender. Drain and place the beans in a baking dish. Heat oil in a saucepan and sauté the onions and garlic lightly. Add tomatoes, parsley, green pepper and cook for a few minutes or until sauce thickens. Remove from heat and pour sauce over the butter beans. Add salt and pepper and bake in moderate oven for about 1 hour. If necessary, add water so that the beans are tender and a little sauce is left. Serve hot or cold.

• Sausages cooked in wine • Stuffed vineleaves • Baked butter beans in tomato sauce

Fried aubergines (Melitzanes tiganites)

5 servings

1 kg aubergines

1 teacup beer

2 teacups flour

Oil for frying

Salt

Wash aubergines and cut into thin slices. Salt and leave in a colander for about an hour to drain. Prepare a thick batter as follows: Mix two cups flour with one cup beer and a little salt. Let batter sit for half an hour. Dip the aubergine slices one by one in the batter and fry in very hot oil. Serve hot or cold with tzatziki or skorthalia. (See page 26.)

Fried courgettes (Kolokythakia tiganita)

5 servings

1 kg large courgettes

1 teacup beer

2 teacups flour

Oil for frying

Salt

Wash and cut courgettes into thin slices. Salt and place in a colander for about an hour to drain. Prepare a thick batter as follows: Mix two cups flour with one cup beer and a little salt. Let batter sit for half an hour. Dip the courgette slices one by one in the batter and fry in very hot oil. Serve hot or cold with tzatziki or skorthalia. (See page 26.)

Fried peppers (Piperies tiganites)

4 servings

1/2 kg long sweet peppers

Oil for frying

Vinegar, salt

Wash peppers well, remove seeds, drain and salt. Heat oil in frying pan and fry the peppers. Turn as soon as they brown. Arrange them on a small plate and sprinkle with vinegar. Serve a day later. A good appetizer with ouzo or wine.

Appetizer plate (Orektika sto piato)

1 serving

1 boiled potato

1 tinned sardine

1 hardboiled egg, 1/2 tomato

2 lettuce leaves, 1 small onion

1 slice ham, 1 slice salami

1 cube feta cheese, 2-3 olives

Peel and slice potato. Spread the lettuce leaves on a plate and arrange on them the sardine, salami, ham, sliced potato, halved egg, sliced tomato, cheese and olives. Put a dab of mayonnaise on the egg and a lemon slice on the sardine. Peel and slice onion, and sprinkle over plate with a little oil.

● **Fried aubergines** ● **Fried courgettes**

About 25-30 pasties

Ingredients for the dough:

500 gr flour

2 level tsps salt

5 tbsps oil

1 tsp baking powder

Water as needed

Filling:

1 kg spinach

250 gr phyllo or puff pastry dough

250 gr feta cheese

1 egg

2 cups oil

4 fresh green onions

Dill

Salt, pepper

Spinach pasties (Spanakopitakia)

C lean and wash spinach. Chop finely. Heat 1 cup of oil in saucepan and sauté the finely chopped onion. Add spinach and dill and cook for a few minutes. Remove from heat, add the eggs, feta, salt and pepper and mix well. Make dough by mixing the ingredients well, adding as much water as necessary to make a dough that is neither too firm nor too soft. Let dough rest for a while. Then roll out and use a tea cup to cut round pieces. Place some filling on each piece, moisten the edges with a little water and press down to seal. Brush pasties with a little oil, place on an oiled baking sheet and bake in moderate oven until well browned. The same filling can be used with phyllo dough. Cut dough in strips 3 in. wide. Brush each strip with oil and place a teaspoon of filling on one end. Fold over into a triangle- shaped pasty. Fry in hot oil.

6 servings

1 kg minced veal

4 slices bread

4-5 tbsps oil

2 eggs

2 onions

3 cloves garlic

4 tbsps vinegar

Oregano, salt, pepper

Oil for frying

Meatballs as appetizers (Keftedes ya meze)

R emove crusts from bread, soak in water and squeeze to remove excess. Mix with minced veal, finely chopped onions, garlic, vinegar, oregano, salt and pepper. Knead well for 5 minutes and leave in frig for an hour. Shape into balls of desired size, flour and fry in hot oil.

• Spinach pasties • Cheese pasties • Meatballs as appetizers

5-6 servings

1-1/2 kg small squid

Salt, pepper

Oil for frying

2 lemons

Fried squid (Kalamarakia tiganita)

Clean the squid by removing the transparent bone. Wash and drain. Heat plenty of oil in a heavy frying pan. Flour the squid well and fry until crisp and golden brown. When all are fried, salt and serve with lemon slices.

4 servings

1/2 kg small whitebait

1/2 teacup flour

Salt, pepper

2 lemons

Oil for frying

Fried whitebait (Marides tiganites)

Wash the fish well without cleaning them. Salt and put aside for half an hour. Put plenty of oil in a deep frying pan. Flour the fish. When the oil is very hot, fry fish until golden brown. Remove with slotted spoon and serve at once. Serve with lemon slices and either green salad or tomato and onion salad.

6-8 servings

1-1/2 kg mussels

3/4 teacup milk

1 cup flour

1 beaten egg

1 tbsp oil

Salt, pepper

Oil for frying

Fried mussels (Mydia tiganita)

Wash mussels well and open with a sharp knife. Remove from shells. Wash and drain well. Mix the egg, milk, oil, salt and pepper. Add the flour and mix well until batter is smooth. Refrigerate batter for about 1 hour. Heat the oil in the frying pan and and dip the mussels one or two at a time into the batter and fry. Serve with salad or as an appetizer.

● Fried squid ● Fried whitebait

Tunafish salad (Tonosalata)

4 servings

1 tin tunafish, 1 tomato

4-5 lettuce leaves

Diced cucumber, green pepper

(2 tbsps each)

1 radish, 5-6 olives,

Oil, lemon

F inely chop tomato, lettuce, cucumber, green pepper and radish. Break up the tunafish. Put all ingredients together with the olives and an oil and lemon dressing.

Potato salad (Patatosalata)

6 servings

1 kg potatoes

1/2 teacup olive oil

1 large onion

Juice of 1 lemon

Finely chopped parsley

Salt, pepper

W ash potatoes well and boil in their skins. Peel and slice. Place in a salad bowl. Slice onion into a bowl, add parsley, oil, salt, pepper and lemon juice and pour over potatoes. Mix ingredients and serve.

Russian salad (Salata rosiki)

4 servings

2 large carrots

2 large potatoes

2 tbsps peas

1 tbsp capers

2 pickled cucumbers

Salt, pepper

6 tbsps mayonnaise

2 or 3 hardboiled eggs

B oil peeled carrots and potatoes and cut into small cubes. Cook peas. Dice cucumbers and place all ingredients in a bowl. Add salt, pepper and mayonnaise. Mix well. Place salad on a platter and garnish with hardboiled eggs.

Aubergine salad (Melitzanosalata)

6 servings

1 kg round aubergines

1 cup olive oil

2-3 cloves garlic, crushed

1 cup mayonnaise

Juice of 1 lemon or vinegar

1 onion   Salt

P rick aubergines with a fork and bake until soft. When cool, peel, chop into bowl and pound to a pulp. Add the crushed garlic and finely chopped onion. Gradually add oil, lemon juice and salt. Beat mixture well and then add mayonnaise.

● **Tunafish salad** ● **Potato salad** ● **Russian salad** ● **Aubergine salad**

Fish roe salad (Taramosalata)

6 servings

150 gr fish roe (tarama)

5 slices of stale bread

1 large onion, grated

Juice of 2 lemons

A few lettuce leaves

2 cups olive oil

P lace the fish roe in a bowl and beat with mixer for a few minutes. Remove crusts from bread, soak bread in water and then squeeze out excess water. Add bread gradually to the fish roe, and then the oil, onion and lemon juice, mixing constantly. Place the lettuce leaves on a platter and serve the taramosalata on top.

Yoghurt dip (Tzatziki)

4 servings

1 cup strained yoghurt

1 medium cucumber

2 (or more) garlic cloves to taste

1 tbsp olive oil

4-5 drops lemon juice

Salt

P eel the cucumber and grate (as for carrots) onto a clean towel. Press to remove juices. Put yoghurt in a bowl, add well-drained cucumber, grated garlic and mix well. To this mixture add the oil, salt and lemon juice. Refrigerate. Serve cold.

Garlic sauce (Skorthalia)

4 servings

4 cloves garlic

1/2 cup olive oil

4 medium potatoes

Vinegar, salt

B oil and peel potatoes. Peel garlic. Place potatoes and garlic in blender and whiz until well mixed. Add the oil gradually, and then a little salt and vinegar. Whiz the mixture for a few seconds. If the oil separates, beat mixture with a little warm water, and it will "bind" again.

Cheese salad (Tirosalata)

4 servings

200 gr manouri, anthotiro or
    other unsalted cheese

150 gr blue cheese

150 gr grated graviera

1 tsp mustard

Few drops of lemon juice

G rate the manouri and place in a bowl. Add the remaining ingredients, mix well and serve garnished with cucumber slices.

● **Fish roe salad** ● **Yoghurt dip** ● **Garlic sauce**

Cheese pasties from Mytilene
(Tiropitakia Mytilinis)

About 25-28 pasties

Ingredients for dough:

500 gr flour

2 level tsps salt

5 tbsps olive oil

1 tsp baking powder

Water as required

Filling:

3 teacups Mytilene cheese

  (ladotiri), grated

3 eggs

1 teacup milk

I n a bowl, put the flour, salt, baking powder and oil and knead. Add as much water as necessary to make dough that is not too firm and not too soft. Set aside and prepare filling. Place the grated cheese in a bowl and mix with the eggs and milk. Roll out the dough and cut round pieces with a teacup. On each circle place a little cheese filling, moisten edges and press to close. Place pasties on a buttered baking sheet and bake in moderate oven until well browned. Serve hot.

Cheese pasties [Tiropitakia (trigona)]

25-30 triangular pasties

250 gr feta cheese

1 teacup grated cheese (graviera)

2 eggs

1/2 teacup milk

1 teacup melted butter

10 sheets phyllo dough

Pinch nutmeg

M ash feta with a fork. Add the grated cheese and eggs. Mix well, add milk and nutmeg. Mix well. Cut each phyllo sheet into 3-4 strips lengthwise. Take one strip, brush with the butter and place a tsp of the mixture on one end. Fold in such a way as to produce a little triangle-shaped pasty. Continue until all the ingredients are used up. Brush tops with butter. Bake pasties on buttered baking sheet in moderate oven.

Spinach pie with cheese

(Spanakopita me tiri)

5-6 servings

1 kg spinach

250 gr feta cheese

2 eggs

8 fresh green onions

1-1/2 teacup oil

Fresh dill

Salt, pepper

250 gr phyllo dough

Blanch spinach for a minute or two and drain well. Heat half the oil in saucepan and sauté the chopped onions. Add spinach and dill and mix well. Remove from heat, adding the eggs, feta, salt and pepper. Mix. Oil a large baking pan 35x40 cm. Place half the sheets of phyllo in the pan, brushing each one with oil before placing the next one on top. Place dough on the bottom in such a way that it comes up over the side of the pan in order to keep the filling in. Spread with the filling. Fold in the overhang from the bottom sheets, and cover with the rest of the phyllo, remembering to oil each sheet. With a sharp knife, score the top two sheets into squares and pour over the remaining oil. Bake pie at about 180°C until well browned, or for about one hour. Equally delicious hot or cold.

salads

Cabbage and carrot salad

(Lahanosalata me karota)

6 servings

1 small cabbage

3 carrots

2 tbsps vinegar

Oil, salt

W ash cabbage and slice thinly with sharp knife. Grate carrots. Mix together in a bowl. Add salt, oil and vinegar to taste.

Red cabbage salad (Kokkino lahano salata)

6-8 servings

1 red cabbage (firm) about 1 kg

Juice of 1 lemon

Salt

1/2 cup olive oil

S lice the cabbage very thinly with a sharp knife. Put in deep salad bowl. Add salt, oil and lemon juice to taste.

String bean salad (Salata ambelofasoula)

6 servings

1-1/4 kg string beans

2 tbsps chopped parsley

1/2 tsp grated garlic

1 tsp chopped onion

1 teacup olive oil

3 tbsps vinegar

C ut around beans to remove strings and wash. Drop beans into boiling, salted water. When tender, remove, drain and put on a platter. Sprinkle the garlic, onion and parsley on top and then pour over the oil and vinegar.

Cauliflower or broccoli salad

(Kounoupidi i brokolo salata)

5-6 servings

1 cauliflower, about 2 kg

1/2 teacup oil

Juice of two lemons

Salt

C ut off cauliflower stem and leaves and wash. Boil in salted water for about 25 minutes or as desired. Drain and place in a salad bowl. Sprinkle over the oil and lemon juice. The same recipe may be used for broccoli.

Boiled green vegetables

(Horta vrasta)

4 servings

1 kg leafy green vegetables

1/3 teacup oil

Juice of 1 lemon

Clean and wash vegetables well. Heat water in a saucepan until it comes to a boil. Then drop in the vegetables. Boil for about 30 minutes or as desired. Drain and pour over oil and lemon. Add salt to taste. Serve hot or cold.

Boiled courgette salad (Kolokythakia salata)

5-6 servings

1 kg small courgettes

1/2 teacup olive oil

Juice of 1 lemon

Salt

A little baking soda

Wash courgettes and cut off ends. Heat salted water with 1/2 tsp soda. The soda keeps the courgettes green. When water is boiling, drop in the courgettes and boil for about 15 minutes. Drain. Place in a bowl, pour over oil and lemon and serve.

Beetroot salad (Pantzaria salata)

4 servings

1 kg beetroot

1/4 teacup oil

2 tbsps vinegar

2 garlic cloves

Salt

Cut the stems and greens from the beetroots. Wash beetroots well and boil in plenty of water for about 20 minutes. Drain. While still hot, cut off the outer skin and slice. Place in a bowl and sprinkle grated garlic on top. Pour over oil, vinegar and add salt. Can also be served with garlic sauce.

Bean salad Biaz (Fasolia salata Biaz)

6 servings

500 gr dried white beans

1 onion, thinly sliced

Chopped parsley

Few black olives

6 tbsps olive oil

Juice of 1 lemon

Wash beans and soak in plenty of cold water overnight. Next day, boil until tender and drain. Place on a platter and add onions, parsley, lemon juice and oil.

Fresh mushroom salad

(Salata me freska manitaria)

6 servings

1 kg fresh mushrooms

2 tbsps olive oil

2 lemons

250 gr tomatoes

1 sweet red pepper

1 green pepper Salt, pepper

Mustard or ketchup

Wash, slice and mix together the tomatoes and peppers. Cut mushrooms in half and place in a bowl with the oil and lemon juice. Pour over the ketchup, salt, pepper and mustard. Mix the mushrooms with the other ingredients and refrigerate for 20-30 minutes before serving.

Lettuce salad (Maroulosalata)

4 servings

1 large lettuce

4 fresh green onions

3-4 sprigs fresh dill

Salt

Lemon juice or vinegar

1/4 teacup oil

Discard any discoloured leaves. Wash and drain lettuce well. Cut up as desired (thinly, coarsely, with sharp knife or with hands). Wash and chop the onions. Chop dill. Mix ingredients in a salad bowl and add salt, oil and lemon juice or vinegar.

Corn cocktail (Kalamboki kokteil)

4 servings

1 tin kernel corn

1 tomato

1 green pepper

2 tbsps diced cucumber

2 radishes

Oil, vinegar, salt

Drain corn well. Place in a bowl. Wash and dice tomato, green pepper and radishes. Mix together, add salt, vinegar and oil.

● **Lettuce salad** ● **Corn cocktail**

6 servings

3 ripe red tomatoes

1 cucumber

1 medium onion

2 green peppers

12 black olives

180 gr feta cheese

1/2 teacup olive oil

2 tbsps vinegar

Oregano, salt

Village salad (Horiatiki salata)

W ash and slice tomatoes and peppers. Peel cucumber and onion and slice. Arrange vegetables in a salad bowl and sprinkle with salt and oregano. Put the olives and feta cheese chunks on top and pour over oil and vinegar.

● **Village salad**

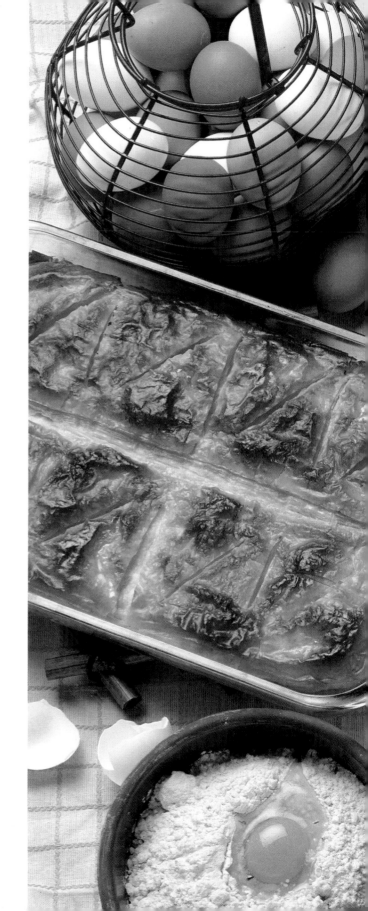

pies

- Cheese pie
- Spinach pie

20 pieces

3 tbsps butter

3 heaping tbsps flour

3 glasses cold milk

300 gr phyllo dough

3 eggs

1 cup melted butter

1 cup grated cheese (graviera)

250 gr feta cheese

Dash of grated nutmeg

Cheese pie (Tiropita sto tapsi)

M elt the butter. Add the flour and stir well with a wooden spoon. Add cold milk and keep stirring until smooth and thick. Remove from heat, add the cheeses and eggs. Mix well. Butter a baking pan and put in half the phyllo dough, buttering each sheet. The phyllo should come up above the top of the pan. Spread the cheese mixture on top and fold over the bottom phyllo sheets. Cover with the remaining phyllo, buttering each sheet. Pour over remaining butter. Score top two sheets of dough with a sharp knife into squares. Bake in moderate oven for about 50-60 minutes.

20-30 pieces

1 kg spinach

1/2 kg phyllo dough

250 gr feta cheese

1-1/2 teacups oil

4-6 fresh green onions

2-3 eggs

4-5 sprigs fresh dill

1 teacup melted butter

Salt

Spinach and cheese pie (Spanakotiropita)

C lean, wash and drain the spinach well. Wash and chop onions, sauté in large pot with a cup of oil. Add spinach and dill. Mix. Remove from heat and add the cheese. Oil a baking pan with the remaining oil. Put in half the phyllo dough, buttering each sheet. The phyllo should come up above the top of the pan. Spread the spinach and cheese mixture on top and fold over the bottom phyllo sheets. Cover with the remaining phyllo, buttering each sheet. Score the top two sheets of dough with a sharp knife. Bake in moderate oven for about 1 hour. Equally delicious hot or cold.

5-6 servings

1/2 kg milk

3 teacups flour

3 eggs

250 gr yoghurt

250 gr butter

350 gr grated graviera cheese

250 gr grated kefalotiri

6 tbsps butter

Salt

Cheese pie from Yannena (Pita yanniotiki)

M ix the flour, yoghurt, eggs and a little salt in a bowl and knead together. Add a little water if necessary. Divide dough into three parts, one larger than the others, and roll out. Place the largest sheet in a buttered baking pan, with pastry coming up the sides of the pan. Butter and add the second sheet, also buttered. Spread over the cheeses, dot with butter and cover with the third sheet of pastry. Pinch edges together. Pour over the remaining butter and score with a sharp knife. Pour over the milk. Bake in preheated oven for about 1 hour or until golden brown.

Note: This dough requires neither baking powder nor yeast.

6 servings

1 kg leeks

4 eggs

Salt, pepper

1 teacup milk

200 gr kefalograviera cheese

2 tbsps finely chopped parsley

500 gr phyllo dough

1 cup butter

Leek pie (Prasopita)

Heat half the butter with the chopped leeks and sauté over medium heat for about 10 minutes. Add the parsley, salt, pepper and remove from heat. In a bowl put the eggs, milk, cubed graviera cheese and leeks and mix well. Butter a baking pan and put in half the phyllo dough, buttering each sheet. The phyllo should come up above the top of the pan. Spread the filling on top and fold over the bottom phyllo sheets. Cover with the remaining phyllo, buttering each sheet. Score top two sheets of dough with a sharp knife into squares. Bake in moderate oven for about 45-50 minutes or until golden brown. Serve hot or cold.

20-30 pieces

1 kg leeks

1 teacup rice

1 litre milk

250 gr yoghurt

6 eggs

800 gr feta cheese

250 gr kefalograviera cheese

1-1/2 teacup butter

1/4 cup oil

1 tsp salt

Dough

1 kg flour

3 tbsps oil

1 tbsp vinegar

Salt and water

Leek pie from Zarohori (Prasopita Zarohori)

Chop leeks. Boil rice in plenty of water for 10 minutes and drain. In a bowl put the eggs, leeks, boiled rice, yoghurt, milk, 1 cup butter and 1/4 cup oil. Add the grated cheeses and mix well. To make the dough, knead the flour with the oil, vinegar, a pinch of salt and as much water as required to make a smooth, soft dough. Roll out dough in six sheets. Butter large baking pan. Put in first sheet of dough and cover with 1/5 the filling. Repeat until all dough and filling are used up, ending with a sheet of dough. Score pie with a sharp knife and pour over remaining butter. Bake pie in pre-heated moderate oven for about 1 hour or until well browned on top.

● Leek pie

5-6 servings

1 kg veal

2 teacups rice

1 teacup butter

250 gr yoghurt

1 medium onion

Dough

4 teacups flour

1 tsp baking powder

2 teacups butter

1 tsp salt

Epirot meat pie (Pita ipeirotiki)

Boil the meat in plenty of water with salt and a little celery. Cook the rice separately in salted water for 15 minutes. Drain. While the meat is cooking, prepare the dough. Mix the flour, baking power, salt and butter in a bowl. Add enough water to make a smooth, soft dough. Cut cooked meat into small pieces. Chop onion, sauté in butter until golden, add the meat and rice. Mix. Remove from heat, add yoghurt and stir lightly. Divide dough into two pieces, one slightly larger than the other. Roll out the larger sheet of dough and place in a buttered pan. The dough should come up over the sides of the pan. Spread the filling over the dough. Roll out the other sheet, butter it and cover the filling. Score and bake in moderately hot oven for about 1 hour.

18-20 pieces

2 kg courgettes

500 gr feta cheese (hard)

300 gr butter

300 gr phyllo dough

3 eggs

Salt, pepper

Cheese and courgette pie

(Pita me tiri ke kolokythia)

Wash and grate courgettes, salt well and leave for half an hour in a colander to drain. Grate the cheese and place in a large bowl. Add the courgettes, eggs, half the butter (melted) and mix lightly. Butter a baking pan and put in half the phyllo dough, buttering each sheet. The phyllo should come up above the top of the pan. Spread the filling on top and fold over the bottom phyllo sheets. Cover with the remaining phyllo, buttering each sheet. Bake in moderate pre-heated oven until well browned and crispy. Serve hot or cold. Note: you can use other kinds of squash in this recipe if desired.

● **Epirot meat pie** ● **Cheese and courgette pie**

4-5 servings

500 gr pork	
1 chopped onion	
1/2 teacup boiled rice	
1 tbsp butter	
1 teacup graviera cheese (cubes)	
Salt, pepper	

Dough

2 teacups flour	
1 teacup butter	
1/2 tsp baking powder	
Water to bind	

Meat pie from Serres (Kreatopita Serron)

M ix the flour, butter and baking powder in a bowl. Add a little salt and enough water to make a smooth dough. Divide the dough into two, one piece slightly larger than the other. Cut the meat into small cubes and sauté with the onion and butter. Add salt, pepper, rice and cheese. Roll out the larger piece of dough and spread in a buttered baking pan to cover the sides as well. Put in meat filling, roll out second sheet of pastry and cover pie. Press together edges. Beat one egg and brush over surface of the pie, score with a sharp knife and bake in moderate oven for about 1 hour.

8 servings

750 gr veal	
12 sheets of phyllo dough	
4 eggs	
12 kg onions	
4 teacups water	
1 teacup milk	
1-1/2 teacup grated cheese	
(graviera or kefalotiri)	
3 tbsps corn flour	
Salt, pepper	
1/2 tsp grated nutmeg	
4 cups butter	

Macedonian meat pie (Pita makedoniki)

C ut the meat and onions into small pieces, wash and bring to boil in a saucepan with 4 cups water. Reduce heat. Simmer until meat is done. Mix the corn flour with the milk and add to saucepan, stirring constantly unitil gravy thickens. Remove pan from heat and when cooled slightly, add the eggs, cheese, salt, pepper and nutmeg. Melt butter, and grease a baking pan. Spread in half the sheets of phyllo, buttering each one. The dough should come up the sides of the pan. Put the filling on top and cover with the remaining phyllo, buttering each one. Score the pie with a sharp knife, pour over any remaining butter and bake in pre-heated moderate oven for about 1 hour.

• **Meat pie from Serres**

6-8 servings

One chicken, about 1-1/2 kg

2 medium onions

3 eggs

1 teacup grated kefalograviera

5 tbsps butter

1/2 kg square noodles

4 eggs

4 teacups flour

1 teacup butter

1 tsp baking powder

Chicken pie from Serres (Kotopita Serron)

B oil chicken. When cool remove meat from bones. Chop onion and sauté in butter. Add chicken. Boil the noodles for 10 minutes in plenty of salted water. Drain. Place in large bowl with the cheese and 3 eggs and mix well. Prepare the pastry as follows: Mix together the flour, baking powder and butter and add enough water to make a smooth dough. Divide into two pieces, one slightly larger than the other. Roll out the larger piece and spread in a buttered baking pan to cover the sides as well. Put on top a layer of noodles, then the sautéed chicken and onions and finally the cubed cheese. Roll out second sheet of pastry and cover chicken. Brush a little beaten egg over the top pastry, score and bake in moderate oven for about 1 hour.

20-30 pieces

500 gr minced beef

3 tbsps butter

1 chopped onion

1 small tin tomatoes

1 tsp cinnamon

1/2 tsp cloves

3 eggs

10 pastry sheets

1 kg courgettes

1 cup grated graviera

4 tbsps butter

Salt, pepper

Courgette and minced beef pie

(Pita me kolokythakia ke kima)

B oil the courgettes, drain and mash. Heat butter in a saucepan and sauté the onions and minced beef. Add the sieved tomatoes, eggs, cheese, cinnamon, cloves, salt, pepper and mashed courgettes. Mix together well. Butter a baking pan and put in half the phyllo dough, buttering each sheet. The phyllo should come up above the top of the pan. Spread the filling on top and fold over the bottom phyllo sheets. Cover with the remaining phyllo, buttering each sheet. Score top two sheets of dough into squares with a sharp knife. Pour over any remaining butter. Bake in moderate oven for about 1 hour.

● **Chicken pie from Serres**

12-14 pieces

3 cups of different cheeses, grated

(including Cypriot haloumi

cheese)

1 cup crumbled feta cheese

1 cup oil

1 cup milk

3 eggs

1 tsp dried mint

3 level tsps baking powder

2-1/2 cups flour

Cypriot cheese pie [Flaouna (tiropita Kyprou)]

P lace all the cheeses in a large bowl, add the oil, mint and egg yolks and stir until well mixed. Put the baking powder with the flour and add to the cheese mixture. Beat the egg whites until stiff and add to mixture. Pour into a buttered baking pan. If desired, brush with egg and sprinkle with sesame seeds. Bake in pre-heated moderate oven for 90 minutes.

6 servings

500 gr self-raising flour

250 gr butter

1 kg potatoes

1 teacup grated graviera

1 clove garlic

1/2 tsp grated nutmeg

1 teacup undiluted evaporated milk

Salt, pepper

Potato pie (Patatopita)

M ix flour, butter, and a little salt in a bowl and add water to make a smooth, soft dough. Divide into two pieces, one bigger than the other. Wash potatoes and boil in plenty of water. While the potatoes are boiling, roll out the larger sheet of dough and spread in a baking pan. The dough should cover all the surface of the buttered pan (including the sides). Peel and mash the boiled potatoes, place in a bowl together with the cheese, milk, salt, pepper, nutmeg and crushed garlic and mix well. Spread on top of the buttered bottom sheet of pastry in the pan. Roll out the second sheet of pastry, butter and place, buttered side up, on top of the potatoes. Bake in pre-heated moderate oven for about 1 hour. Cool before serving.

6 servings

500 gr veal

250 gr pork

1 large onion

1 teacup cheese, cubed

1/2 tsp ground cloves

3 tbsps oil

Dough

300 gr flour

150 gr butter

Pinch salt

1/4 tsp baking powder

Beef and pork pie

(Pita me moscharisio ke hirino kreas)

M ix butter and flour, add salt, baking powder and enough water to make a smooth, soft dough. Divide in two pieces, one piece a little larger than the other. In a saucepan, sauté the cubed meat and onions in the oil. When cooked, remove from heat, add cloves, salt, pepper and cheese. Mix well. Roll out the larger sheet of dough and place in a buttered baking pan; it should cover the sides of the pan. Spread over the filling. Roll out the second sheet to cover the filling and brush with butter. Score with sharp knife and bake in pre-heated moderate oven for about 1 hour. Cool slightly before cutting.

soups

- Chickpea soup
- Bean soup
- Lentil soup

Chickpea soup (Soupa revithia)

4 servings

1/2 kg dried chickpeas

2 finely chopped onions

1 teacup oil

Juice of 1 lemon

Salt, pepper

S oak the chickpeas overnight in water. Next day rinse well. Place the oil and onions in saucepan and sauté. Add the chickpeas, salt, pepper and cold water to cover. Simmer for about 1 hour, adding water if necessary, or until tender. Serve hot with lemon juice.

Bean soup (Fasolia soupa)

6 servings

1/2 kg dried white beans

1 teacup oil

1 large onion

1 tin peeled tomatoes

2 medium carrots

1/2 cup celery leaves

Salt, pepper

1 small hot pepper (optional)

W ash the beans and place in a saucepan with plenty of water. Boil for about half an hour and then add the oil, chopped onions, carrots and celery, salt and pepper. Simmer for about 1 hour or until beans are tender. Serve hot with olives, pickles or smoked herring.

Lentil soup (Soupa fakes)

4-5 servings

1/2 kg lentils

1/2 kg tomatoes

4 garlic cloves, 2 onions

2-3 bayleaves

Salt, pepper

1 teacup oil

Vinegar (optional)

W ash lentils and place in saucepan with plenty of water. Add the onion, garlic, oil and tomatoes and boil for about 1 hour or until lentils are tender. Serve hot or cold with olives and pickles.

Tahini soup (Tahinosoupa)

4 servings

1-1/2 teacup pasta

8 glasses water

12 tsps tahini (sesame seed butter)

1 tsp lemon juice

Salt, pepper

H eat a pot with the water, salt and pepper. When boiling, add the pasta (whatever you prefer, usually elbow macaroni), stir and then boil 15-20 minutes. Dilute the tahini in a bowl with a little cold water, remove soup from heat and add the tahini and the lemon juice. Serve hot.

Country-style or spring
vegetable soup (Soupa horiatiki i anixiatiki)

4 servings

2 large potatoes, 2 carrots

1 tbsps dried beans

2 medium courgettes, 2 onions

1/2 kg cabbage

1 tbsps elbow macaroni

1 small tin tomatoes

1 beef cube

1/2 cup butter

B oil beans until tender. Peel potatoes and carrots and dice. Slice the onion and cabbage. Place all together with the butter in a large pot. Add the tomatoes, beef cube and plenty of water. When vegetables are done, add the beans and macaroni and boil for another 10-15 minutes. If desired, sprinkle a little grated kefalotiri on each plate of soup when serving.

Onion soup (Kremmydosoupa)

4 servings

500 gr onions

3 heaping tbsps butter

2 tbsps corn flour

6 teacups beef or chicken stock

1 bayleaf, 1 clove garlic

4 slices bread, toasted

2 tbsps grated kefalotiri or

　parmesan cheese

P eel and rinse onions, slice and sauté in butter until golden. Add corn flour, stock, a little salt, pepper and simmer soup for about half an hour. When it is cooked, pour into four individual baking dishes, grate the garlic over the soup. Put a slice of toast in each bowl, trimming to fit if necessary. Sprinkle grated cheese over the toast and place the dishes in the oven until cheese melts. Serve piping hot. Very good on cold winter days.

Vegetable soup (Hortosoupa)

4-5 servings

3 medium potatoes

1 onion

3 medium carrots

2 stalks celery

2 small courgettes

1/2 cup oil or butter

6 cups water

Juice of 1 lemon

Salt, pepper

P eel, wash and dice the potatoes and carrots. Wash and dice courgettes. Chop celery, onion and tomatoes and place all vegetables in a pot with the water. Add the oil or butter and simmer. When done, remove from heat, add lemon juice and stir.

Leek soup (Prasosoupa)

4 servings

1/2 kg leeks

2 carrots

1 tbsp corn flour

2 potatoes

1 cube beef stock

1/2 cup butter

Peel, wash and chop the leeks, carrots and potatoes. Put leeks in a pot with butter and sauté until golden, stirring constantly. Add the corn flour, stir, and add the stock cube, carrots, potatoes and about 1 litre of water. Simmer until vegetables are tender. Serve soup hot as is, or whiz in blender.

Tomato soup (Soupa domata)

4 servings

1/4 cup butter

2 carrots

1 medium onion

1 tbsp corn flour

1/2 kg tomatoes or 1 large tin

1 tbsp celery leaves

1 cube chicken stock

Salt, pepper, pinch sugar

Heat butter in a pot and sauté finely chopped onion. Add corn flour mixed with cold water and stir for one minute. Add the tomatoes and stock cube, together with 5 cups water, chopped carrots and celery, salt, pepper and sugar and simmer until vegetables are tender. Remove from heat and sieve soup or whiz in blender. If you wish, add a little finely chopped sweet basil.

Beef and vegetable soup

(Soupa me kreas vodino)

4-6 servings

1 kg beef

1/2 kg potatoes

1/4 kg carrots

3 onions

4 courgettes

2 tbsps celery leaves

3 tomatoes

Salt, pepper   1/3 cup oil

Cut meat into portions and place in large pot with water to boil. Add salt and pepper. Peel the potatoes, carrots and onions and put, together with the diced courgettes, into pot with the meat. Add the celery. Quarter tomatoes and add to soup. When the meat is done, serve the soup in bowls with the meat and vegetables.

Pasta soup (Trahanas soupa xini)

4 servings

1 teacup trahanas

 (type of country-style pasta)

2 tbsps butter

4 cups water, salt

Heat the water and butter in a saucepan. Add the trahanas and salt. Boil for 15-20 minutes. If you wish, add egg and lemon with 2 eggs and the juice of 1 lemon.

● **Leek soup** ● **Tomato soup**

Potato soup (Patatosoupa)

4 servings

1/4 cup butter

1/2 kg potatoes

2-3 carrots

1 medium onion

1 cube chicken stock (optional)

2 tbsps celery

Salt, pepper

3-4 tbsps fresh cream (optional)

Peel and slice potatoes. Place in pot with the butter and onion and sauté for 5 minutes. Add carrots and celery. Stir and sayté for a few minutes. Add water and the cube. Reduce heat, and simmer soup for 25-30 minutes. Add the cream, if desired.

Carrot soup (Soupa apo karota)

4 servings

1/4 cup butter

1 medium onion

1/2 kg carrots

1 tbsp parsley

1/2 tsp sugar

1 cube chicken stock (optional)

Salt, pepper

Peel and grate carrots. Chop onion and parsley. Melt butter in a saucepan and cook carrots and onion for 5 minutes. Add 5 cups water and the cube if desired. Reduce heat and simmer soup for about half an hour. Add the parsley, salt, pepper and sugar.

Chicken soup with egg and lemon
(Kotosoupa avgholemono)

6 servings

1 chicken, about 2 kg

1 teacup rice

2 eggs

Juice of 2 lemons

1/4 teacup butter

1 small onion (optional)

1 carrot (optional)

8 cups water

Salt, pepper

Clean and wash chicken. In a large pot, boil chicken in 8 cups of water, skimming off the foam. Add butter, onion, carrot and salt. Boil until chicken is tender. Remove chicken and vegetables to a platter. Add rice to the stock and boil for 20 minutes. Beat the eggs well. Add lemon juice, beating constantly, and then gradually add some of the hot stock. Remove soup from heat. Pour egg mixture into the soup, stirring vigorously.

● **Potato soup** ● **Carrot soup**

Mushroom soup (Soupa manitaria)

4 servings

1 tbsp butter

1 small onion, grated

250 gr fresh mushrooms

2 tbsps corn flour

1 cube chicken stock (optional)

1 bayleaf

3 tbsps cream

1 carrot

1 tbsp celery

Melt butter in saucepan, add the sliced mushrooms and onion. Cover and cook for about 5 minutes. Then add the corn flour and stir for 2 minutes until dissolved. Add the stock cube, diced carrot, celery and bayleaf and 5 cups water. Simmer for about 20 minutes. Remove bayleaf, take the pan off the heat and add the cream. If you haven't any cream, undiluted evaporated milk can also be used.

Country-style pea soup
(Soupa horiatiki me xera bizelia)

5 servings

1/2 kg dried peas

2 carrots

2 leeks

4 rashers bacon

4 tbsps butter

Salt, pepper

1 tbsp celery leaves

Clean peas and place in bowl with cold water to soak for about 2 hours. Peel, wash and chop the carrots, celery and leeks. Cut bacon and fry in butter, then add the vegetables. Drain peas and place in a pot with water. As soon as the peas begin to boil, add the vegetables, salt and pepper and simmer until done. Serve hot.

Meatball soup with egg-lemon sauce
(Youvarlakia soupa avgolemono)

5 servings

1/2 kg minced beef

1/2 cup rice

1 onion

3 eggs

2 tbsps oil

Juice of 1 lemon

Chopped dill or mint

1/4 cup butter

Salt, pepper

Mix the minced meat, onion, 1 egg, rice, dill or mint, oil, salt and pepper. Knead well for a few minutes, and shape into small balls. Place 7 cups water in a large pot with the butter and bring to a boil. Drop in the meatballs, cover and simmer for about 30 minutes. Beat the other two eggs lightly in a bowl, add the lemon juice, continue beating and add some of the hot soup. Remove soup from heat. Put the egg-lemon mixture back into the pot and stir well. Serve hot.

● Mushroom soup

Fishermen's soup or Greek bouillabaisse (Soupa tou psara i kakavia)

8 servings

1 kg rock fish
3 onions
4 ripe tomatoes
4-5 medium potatoes
5-6 carrots
2 cloves garlic
1 tsp dried thyme
1/2 cup ouzo
1 teacup oil
Salt, pepper

C lean the fish and wash well. Peel and chop potatoes, carrots and tomatoes. Heat the oil in a large pot and sauté chopped onion and garlic. Add potatoes, carrots, tomatoes, thyme, fish and ouzo. Add plenty of water and boil. When fish are done, remove from pot, sieve the boiled vegetables, bone the fish and return vegetables and fish to the pot. Serve hot.

Easter soup [Soupa paschalini (mayiritsa)]

6 servings

Heart, liver, lungs and
sweetbreads from one lamb
6 fresh green onions
1 lettuce
2-3 sprigs fresh dill
1 tbsp parsley
1/2 teacup rice
Juice of 2 lemons
2 tbsps corn flour
3 eggs
Salt, pepper
1/2 teacup butter
10 cups water

B lanch the organs in a large pot of boiling water. Drain, cool and chop coarsely. In the same pot, sauté the butter, meat, dill, parsley and chopped onions. Add water and boil for about 20 minutes. Put in the rice and simmer for another 20 minutes. Prepare the egg and lemon (avgholemono). Beat eggs, add lemon juice gradually, still beating. Add a little hot soup, mix and remove pot from heat. Turn the egg-lemon mixture into the soup, stirring vigorously. Serve hot.

pasta

- Baked macaroni
  with minced meat
- Noodles au gratin

Baked macaroni with minced meat

(Pastitsio me macaronia)

8 servings

500 gr macaroni

500 gr minced beef

2 medium onions

1 tin peeled tomatoes

1 teacup butter

3 eggs

1 teacup grated cheese

8 level tbsps flour

4 teacups cold milk

Salt, pepper

1/2 tsp ground nutmeg

S auté the minced beef in the chopped onion with 2 tbsps butter. Add salt, pepper, nutmeg and sieved tomatoes and cook for about 45 minutes. Boil macaroni in plenty of salted water for 15 minutes. Drain and prepare the white sauce as follows: Melt 6 tbsps butter in a saucepan. Add the flour, stirring with wooden spoon, and cold milk. Cook and stir until mixture boils and thickens. Remove from heat, add salt and pepper. Beat the eggs and add to the white sauce together with half the grated cheese. Butter a baking pan, put in half the macaroni, sprinkle with a little grated cheese and spread the minced meat mixture over it. Put the remaining macaroni on top and cover with the white sauce. Spread with a knife. Sprinkle with the remaining grated cheese and bake in moderate oven for about 45 minutes or until golden brown.

Noodles au gratin (Lazania ograten)

6 servings

500 gr noodles

6 tbsps butter

6 level tbsps flour

2 teacups milk

6 tbsps grated cheese

3 eggs

Salt, pepper

1/2 tsp ground nutmeg

B oil the noodles in plenty of salted water for 10 minutes. Drain and cool. Prepare the white sauce: Melt 6 tbsps butter in a saucepan. Add the flour, stirring with wooden spoon. Cook and stir until mixture is smooth. Add cold milk, and continue stirring until mixture thickens. Remove from heat. Beat the eggs and add to the white sauce together with the grated cheese, salt, pepper and nutmeg. Pour white sauce over the noodles, mix, place in buttered baking dish and bake until top is golden brown.

Macaroni from Rhodes (Makaronia Rodou)

4 servings

500 gr spaghetti

6 tbsps butter

6 tbsps oil

2 large aubergines

6 tbsps grated cheese

200 gr minced beef

1 medium onion

Salt, pepper

1 bayleaf

1/2 tin peeled tomatoes

B oil spaghetti as usual, drain and cool. Meantime, peel and slice the aubergines. Fry sliced aubergines in hot oil. Sauté chopped onion and add to minced meat with the bayleaf, salt, pepper and half the tomatoes and cook for about 30 minutes. Butter a baking dish, arrange the aubergines on the bottom layer, the macaroni next, then the remaining cheese and last the minced meat mixture. Cover with the remaining tomatoes, sieved. Bake in moderate oven for about 30 minutes. Serve hot.

Bow-knot macaroni (Makaronia fiongakia)

5-6 servings

500 gr bow-knot macaroni

1 small tin peeled tomatoes

1 small tin mushrooms

6 slices ham

1/2 teacup butter

1 clove garlic

1 bayleaf

Salt, pepper

1 teacup grated cheese

B oil the macaroni in plenty of salted water and drain. In another pot, heat two tbsps butter and brown the garlic. Add bayleaf and sieved tomatoes. Slice mushrooms and ham in strips and add to tomatoes with salt and pepper and simmer for a few minutes. Put the remaining butter in a pan and add the macaroni and sauce. Stir well. Serve with grated cheese.

Green tagliatelle with mushrooms
(Taliatelles prasines me manitaria)

5 servings

500 gr green tagliatelle

1 small tin mushrooms

1 onion

1 teacup undiluted evap. milk

1/2 teacup butter

1 teacup grated cheese

Salt

S auté the onion in butter until golden. Sieve mushrooms and add to pan with a little water and milk and let the sauce simmer until thick. Meantime, boil the tagliatelle in lots of salted water for 10 minutes, drain, serve on a platter and pour over the sauce. Serve with grated cheese.

Spaghetti with minced meat sauce

(Macaronia me kima)

6 servings

500 gr spaghetti

500 gr minced beef

1 onion

6 tbsps butter

1 small tin peeled tomatoes

1 bayleaf

Salt, pepper

P ut one tbsp butter in a pan with the chopped onion and sauté. Add minced meat and sauté. Add salt, pepper, bayleaf and tomato. Simmer sauce for about 1 hour. Boil macaroni as usual in plenty of salted water for 15 minutes. Drain, add butter. Serve macaroni on a platter, pour over the meat sauce and sprinkle with grated cheese.

Square noodles from Metsovo

(Hilopites Metsovou)

5 servings

1 kg square noodles

1 teacup grated kefalotiri

1 teacup butter

Tomato sauce

Salt, pepper

P ut plenty of salted water in a large pot and bring to boil. Add the noodles and stir until cooked (about 15 minutes). Drain and return to pot. Add the butter and mix well. Serve with tomato sauce and grated cheese.

Baked macaroni (Makaronia fournou)

6 servings

1/2 kg macaroni

1 small tin mushrooms

6 slices ham

3 tbsps peas

1/2 teacup butter

3 teacups cold milk

3 eggs,

Salt, pepper

1/2 tsp ground nutmeg

6 tbsps grated cheese

B oil the macaroni in plenty of salted water for 10 minutes. Drain and place in buttered baking pan. Slice mushrooms and ham and add the cooked peas. Mix with the macaroni. Melt butter in a saucepan. Add flour and mix well. Add the cold milk and stir until mixture comes to a boil. Remove from heat, add salt, pepper, nutmeg, beaten eggs and half the grated cheese and mix well. Pour this sauce over the macaroni and mix well. Sprinkle with remaining grated cheese. Bake in moderate oven for 20-25 minutes.

● **Spaghetti with minced meat sauce** ● **Square noodles from Metsovo**

Pot roast with spaghetti (Corfu)
(Pastitsatha Kerkyras)

6 servings

1 kg veal

1-1/2 teacups peeled tomatoes

1/2 cup dry red wine

5 onions

4 cloves garlic

1/2 teacup butter

1/2 kg spaghetti

6 tbsps grated cheese

1/2 teacup oil

Salt, pepper

Cut garlic cloves in half and insert in the meat at various points with a sharp knife. Salt and pepper meat. Place in a heavy pot with butter and finely chopped onions and sauté. Add wine, sieved tomatoes and a little water. Simmer for about 1 hour. Boil spaghetti in plenty of salted water. Serve the meat, cut into servings, with the spaghetti. Pour over the sauce and sprinkle with grated cheese.

Baked macaroni with meat
(Youvetsi kritharaki)

5 servings

1 kg veal

1/2 kg macaroni

1 tin peeled tomatoes

1 teacup oil

1 teacup grated cheese (kefalotiri)

Salt, pepper

Wash and cut meat into five servings. Place in a pan with the oil and sauté. Add water and cook for about 1 hour. Cook macaroni in plenty of salted water, drain. Place in buttered baking dishes. Divide cooked meat and sauce among baking dishes. Sprinkle with grated cheese. Bake in pre-heated moderate oven until cheese is browned. Serve immediately.

● Pot roast with spaghetti (Corfu) ● Baked macaroni with meat

Spinach and rice with eggs

(Rizi pilafi me spanaki ke avga)

6 servings

1 kg spinach

1 teacup butter

1 teacup rice

6 eggs

6 rashers bacon

6 slices bread

Milk, salt, pepper

C lean and wash spinach. Chop and place in a sauce-pan with a little water. Boil for 5 minutes. Drain. Place 2 tbsps butter in a frying pan and sauté the spinach, adding a little salt, pepper and milk. Simmer. In another saucepan, boil the rice in 3 cups salted water with half the butter. Reduce heat and simmer for about 20 minutes. Put half the rice in a round mould and cover with half the spinach. Repeat. Fry the bacon, the bread slices and then the eggs. Turn out the rice and spinach onto a platter and surround with the fried bread. Place a fried egg and rasher of bacon on each one.

Elbow macaroni in tomato sauce

[Macaronaki kofto (atomiko)]

5 servings

1/2 kg elbow macaroni

1/2 teacup oil

1 onion, 1 clove garlic

1 small tin peeled tomatoes

Salt, pepper, sweet basil

1/2 teacup butter

250 gr grated parmesan or
  kefalotiri

C hop onion and garlic. Sauté in oil, add basil and sieved tomatoes. Salt, pepper and allow the sauce to simmer. Boil the macaroni in plenty of salted water for 15 minutes and drain. Mix the macaroni with butter and divide among 5 individual baking dishes. Pour over sauce, sprinkle with grated cheese and bake for about 10 minutes until the cheese melts.

Rice with vermicelli (Cyprus)

[Rizi pilafi me fide (Kyprou)]

4 servings

1 teacup rice

4 "nests" of vermicelli

3 tbsps butter

1 tsp salt

H eat butter in a saucepan and add vermicelli. Stir and sauté. Add rice, salt and 3 cups water or chicken stock. Stir lightly and simmer for about 20-25 minutes.

● **Spinach and rice with eggs**

sauces

- White sauce
- Mayonnaise
- Tomato sauce
- Piquant sauce with yoghurt
- Yoghurt and beetroot sauce

White sauce (Saltsa besamel)

6 tbsps butter

6 tbsps flour

2 eggs

1 tsp salt

Pepper, ground nutmeg

2 teacups cold milk

Heat butter in a saucepan, add the flour and brown lightly. Add the cold milk, stirring constantly until sauce is thick. Remove from heat, add beaten eggs, salt, pepper and nutmeg.

Mayonnaise (Saltsa mayoneza)

2 egg yolks

1 teacup oil

1 tsp mustard

1/2 tsp salt

Few drops vinegar

Few drops lemon juice

1/2 tsp corn flour

Beat egg yolks with mixer and add salt, mustard, corn flour and 1/2 tsp vinegar. Beat well with mixer, adding the oil bit by bit. When the oil is used up, add the lemon juice little by little. Serve with seafood and fish.

Tomato sauce (Saltsa domata)

1 large tin peeled tomatoes

2 cloves garlic

1/2 tsp sugar

1/2 cup oil

2 onions

1 bayleaf

Pinch of thyme, oregano

Salt, pepper

Peel onions, slice and sauté in saucepan with the oil. Add garlic, thyme, bayleaf, oregano, sugar and chopped tomatoes. Cook for a few minutes. Add salt and pepper and cook for 15- 20 minutes more. Serve the sauce with pasta, rice, chips or fried aubergines.

Piquant sauce with yoghurt

(Saltsa pikantiki me yaourti)

1 teacup yoghurt

1/2 teacup mayonnaise

2 tbsps finely chopped red pepper

1 chopped onion

2 chopped cucumber pickles

Mix the yoghurt with the mayonnaise and half the ingredients. Put the mixture in a bowl and add remaining ingredients. This sauce is good for green salad, boiled vegetables, meat and fish.

Yoghurt and beetroot sauce

(Saltsa me yaourti ke pantzaria)

1 teacup yoghurt

1 heaping tbsp chopped beetroots

1 tbsp capers

1 tbsp grated onion

Place all ingredients in a bowl and mix well. Serve this sauce with fried or grilled fish, meat and even with potato salad.

Egg and lemon sauce (Avgholemono)

Juice of 2 lemons

2 eggs

1 cup hot stock from soup or stew

Beat eggs with a fork in a bowl, add the lemon juice while beating constantly. Then add a few tablespoons of the hot stock little by little, still beating. Pour egg mixture back into pot with the soup or stew. Remove from heat and allow to stand until sauce thickens. Sauce should not boil as the egg will curdle.

eggs

- Omelette (Andros)
- Scrambled eggs
  with tomato
- Eggs with spinach

4-5 servings

2 country-style pork sausages

4 rashers bacon

1/2 kg potatoes

1 tsp salt, pepper

6 eggs, pinch dried mint

2 tbsps butter

Omelette (Andros) (Andriotiki omeleta)

S lice sausages and place in frying pan with butter and chopped bacon. Brown. In another frying pan, fry potatoes and add to the sausages together with beaten eggs, mint, salt and pepper. Fry on one side and then turn over to cook on the other. Serve hot.

2 servings

4 eggs

1 tbsp evaporated milk

Oil, salt, pepper

1 tomato

Scrambled eggs with tomato

(Avga strapatsata)

C hop tomato. Break eggs into a bowl, add tomato, salt and pepper and beat well. Heat oil in frying pan and pour in egg mixture. Cook until done.

4 servings

4 eggs

1 kg spinach

6 tbsps butter

3 tbsps grated cheese (kefalotiri)

Salt, pepper

Eggs with spinach (Avga me spanaki)

C lean and wash spinach well. Boil in a little water and drain. Chop finely. Heat a little butter in a frying pan and sauté spinach. Cover and cook. Add the remaining butter, salt, pepper and grated cheese. With a spoon, make four holes in the spinach and break an egg into each. Cover pan and cook until eggs are done.

Eggs with chicken livers

(Avga me sikotakia poulion)

4 servings

250 gr chicken livers

4 tbsps oil

1 medium onion, sliced

1 chopped green pepper

1 garlic clove (optional)

4 tbsps dry white wine

1 teacup tomato juice

4 eggs

Salt, pepper

Cut the chicken livers into small pieces, wash and drain. Heat oil in frying pan and fry the chicken livers. Salt, pepper and add the onion, green pepper, garlic (if desired) and tomato juice. Cover pan and cook for 15-20 minutes. When sauce is thick, break the eggs one by one into the pan. Cover again and leave to cook for another 5 minutes until eggs are done.

Eggs with buttermilk (Cretan speciality) [Anthogala me avga (specialite Kritis)]

3 servings

3 tbsps buttermilk

6 eggs

Salt, pepper

Pour the buttermilk into a frying pan and cook for 5-6 minutes. Beat the eggs into a bowl, pour into the frying pan with salt and pepper and stir constantly until done.

Ham and cheese sandwiches with eggs (Ta avga tis oras)

4 servings

8 slices bread

4 slices graviera cheese

4 eggs

4 slices ham

1 teacup milk

Salt, pepper

Remove crusts from bread. On each slice of bread place one piece each of ham and cheese. Cover with another slice of bread to make four sandwiches. Heat oil in frying pan. Put milk in bowl, dip sandwiches in it, and then fry until brown on both sides. Finally, fry the eggs in the same oil and put one on top of each sandwich. Serve hot.

Omelette with potatoes and shrimps

(Omeleta me patates ke garides)

4 servings

1/2 kg potatoes

5 rashers bacon

250 gr shrimp, boiled

2 tbsps butter

4 eggs

Salt, pepper, oil

Chopped parsley

P eel and slice potatoes. Fry in lots of oil until golden. Remove from pan and set aside. Peel shrimp and cut in two. Heat the butter in a frying pan and add the fried potatoes, shrimp, bacon, beaten eggs, parsley, salt and pepper. Fry on one side and then turn over and fry on the other. Serve hot.

Baked omelette (Omeleta fournou)

2 servings

4 eggs

1 potato

1 tomato

1 onion

1 courgette

1 sausage

1 tbsp butter

Oil, salt, pepper

1 tbsp grated cheese

P eel onion and potato. Wash courgette. Slice vegetables. Heat oil in frying pan and sauté them until golden brown. Add the chopped tomato. Beat eggs in a bowl. Cut up sausage, fry and add to eggs. Then turn all other ingredients into the bowl and mix well. Butter a baking dish 14-16 cm diameter and pour in ingredients. Bake in preheated moderate oven for about 10 minutes. Serve warm.

● **Baked omelette** ● **Omelette with potatoes and shrimps**

Country-style omelette (Omeleta horiatiki)

6 servings

7 eggs

2 kg potatoes

200 gr bacon

4 tbsps butter

Oil, salt, pepper

1 onion

Peel and slice potatoes. Fry in plenty of oil until golden. Remove from pan. Chop bacon and onions and sauté. Heat a little butter and oil in another frying pan and put in the potatoes, bacon, onion, beaten eggs, salt and pepper. Fry first on one side and then on the other. Serve hot.

Poached eggs Greek-style

(Avga ala ellinika)

4 servings

4 eggs

2 peeled tomatoes

1 medium onion

2 slices ham

1 tbsp flour

1/2 cup sweet red wine

2 tbsps grated cheese

4 slices of graviera cheese

Few drops lemon juice

Cut tomatoes in two. Butter a large baking dish and place tomatoes in it. Chop onion and sauté in a little butter. Add chopped ham and flour, stirring constantly. Add salt, pepper, wine, and grated cheese and mix well. Pour over tomatoes. Bake in moderate oven for 10 minutes and poach eggs as follows: fill a shallow pan with 3 cups water and a few drops lemon. When water boils, break the eggs carefully, one at a time, into the boiling water. As soon as the egg is covered by the white, remove with slotted spoon and place one egg on top of each tomato half. Put a slice of graviera on top of each egg and return to oven until cheese melts.

● **Country-style omelette** ● **Poached eggs Greek style**

vegetables

- Spinach and rice
- Mixed baked vegetables
- Stuffed aubergines
  in tomato sauce

6 servings

2 kg spinach

1 teacup rice

1-1/2 cup oil

3 fresh green onions

Juice of 1 lemon

3-4 sprigs fresh dill

Salt, pepper

Spinach and rice (Spanakorizo)

C lean and wash spinach. Wash and chop onions. Sauté in the oil. Add the spinach and stir for a few minutes. Add 2 cups water and cook for 15 minutes. Then add the rice, dill, lemon juice, salt and pepper and simmer for another 15-20 minutes. Serve hot or cold, with olives or feta cheese.

4 servings

4 courgettes

2 onions

1 kg potatoes

2 cloves garlic

1 tsp chopped parsley

1 teacup oil

Salt, pepper

Mixed baked vegetables (Briam)

P eel the potatoes and onions. Wash courgettes. Slice vegetables and place in a baking dish. Add salt, pepper, finely chopped garlic, onions and parsley. Pour over the oil and 2 cups water, cover with aluminium foil and bake in moderate oven for about 1 hour. Serve with feta cheese or olives.

4 servings

8 aubergines

1/2 kg sliced onions

1 small tin tomatoes

2 teacups oil

6 garlic cloves

Chopped parsley

1/2 tsp sugar

Stuffed aubergines in tomato sauce
(Imam baildi)

C ut the ends of aubergines and wash. Make a lengthwise incision in each one. Heat a cup of oil in a frying pan and sauté the aubergines one by one. Then prepare the stuffing as follows: Put the remaining oil in a saucepan and sauté the onions until golden. Add the garlic, parsley and sieved tomato, mix well and cook for 10 minutes. Remove from heat. With a spoon, open the aubergines and fill with the onion mixture. Place in a baking dish. Pour over remaining sauce and a little water. Bake in moderate oven for 1 hour. Serve hot or cold.

Scalloped potatoes au gratin

(Patates gratine)

4 servings

750 gr boiled potatoes

1 teacup grated cheese

2 cups milk

2 eggs

Salt, pepper

Peel and slice potatoes. Butter a baking dish, arrange potatoes in layers and sprinkle with salt, pepper and cheese. Beat the eggs with the milk and pour over potatoes. Bake in moderate oven for about half an hour or until cooked.

Stewed potatoes in tomato sauce

(Patates yachni)

6 servings

1-1/2 kg potatoes

1-1/2 teacup oil

2 medium onions

1 clove garlic

1 small tin tomatoes

Chopped parsley

Oil for frying

Salt, pepper

Peel potatoes, cut in small pieces and fry lightly. Chop onion and garlic and place in a saucepan with the oil, salt, pepper, parsley, tomato and a little water. Cook the sauce for 15 minutes and add the potatoes. Cook for another 30 minutes.

Fresh broad beans with tomato

(Koukia freska yachni)

4 servings

1 kg fresh broad beans

1-1/2 teacup oil

Dill, salt, pepper

8 fresh green onions

4 ripe tomatoes

Clean the broad beans by cutting the ends, wash and put into a saucepan with the oil, chopped onions, dill, salt and pepper. Sauté until onions are golden. Chop tomatoes and add to pan with a little water and cook for about an hour.

Yellow lentils with oil and lemon

(Fava me ladi ke lemoni)

4 servings

500 gr yellow lentils

1/2 teacup oil

1 small onion

Juice of one lemon

Salt, pepper

5 teacups water

Wash lentils well and drain. Put 5 teacups water in a saucepan. Add the lentils and simmer over low heat for about 30 minutes. When they have thickened, remove from heat and stir with wooden spoon until the lentils become a smooth paste. Add the oil and lemon and continue stirring. Serve hot or cold with a little chopped onion.

4 servings

1 cauliflower, about 1-1/2 kg

3 onions

1 small tin peeled tomatoes

2 teacups oil

Salt, pepper

Stewed cauliflower (Kounoupidi yachni)

Wash cauliflower and cut into small pieces. Place chopped onions in a saucepan with the oil and sauté lightly. Add tomatoes, salt and pepper. Boil for 15 minutes, then add cauliflower and a little water. Cook until cauliflower is tender and the sauce thick.

5-6 servings

1-1/2 kg fresh broad beans

6 artichokes

1 cup oil

6 fresh green onions

1 tin peeled tomatoes

1 tbsp finely chopped dill

Salt, pepper

Artichokes with fresh broad beans

(Anginares me koukia freska)

Clean the beans by cutting around the sides to remove the strings. Usually the hulls are tender and are cooked together with the beans. Clean the artichokes by removing tough leaves and cutting off 1 inch from the top. Remove choke and peel base all around. Place cleaned artichokes in water with lemon juice to prevent discolouring. Chop onions, put in saucepan with the oil and sauté. Add the sieved tomato, the beans and artichokes, dill, salt, pepper and a little water. Cover pan and simmer for about an hour.

4-5 servings

8 artichokes

3 lemons

6 fresh onions

1/2 kg small potatoes

4-5 carrots

1 cup olive oil

Few sprigs dill

Salt, pepper

1 level tbsp flour

2 teacups water

Artichokes with carrots and potatoes

(Anginares ala polita)

Remove tough leaves from the artichokes and cut off about half an inch of the sharp tops. Cut in half. Remove the fuzzy choke and peel around the base. When cleaning each one, rub with lemon to prevent discolouring. Place the cleaned artichokes in a bowl with water to cover and add flour. Cut the potatoes and carrots into large pieces. Heat oil and sauté onions, then add the artichokes, carrots, potatoes, salt and 2 teacups water. Simmer for about an hour until the sauce is thick.

● Stewed cauliflower ● Artichokes with carrots and potatoes

Fresh beans in tomato sauce
(Fasolakia freska yiachni)

4-5 servings

1 kg runner beans

2 medium onions

5-6 tomatoes

1 red pepper (optional)

1 teacup oil

Salt, pepper

Clean the beans, wash and place in saucepan with the chopped onion and oil. Sauté stirring from time to time. Add the chopped tomatoes together with the red pepper, salt, pepper and a little water. Cook over low heat for about an hour.

Peas (Arakas)

5 servings

1 kg shelled peas

2-3 potatoes

1 teacup oil

6 fresh green onions

3-4 sprigs finely chopped dill

1 small tin peeled tomatoes

Salt, pepper

Wash the peas. Place oil in saucepan together with the onion, peas and coarsely chopped potatoes and sauté. Add dill, sieved tomatoes, salt, pepper and a little water. Boil for about one hour or until vegetables are tender. Serve hot or cold.

Okra in tomato sauce (Bamies latheres)

4-5 servings

1 kg okra

1 teacup oil

2 onions, finely chopped

1 clove garlic

5 tomatoes (or 1 small tin) peeled,

　or one tsp tomato paste

Salt, pepper

Prepare the okra by cutting off tough part around stems and wash well. Heat oil in a saucepan and sauté onions and garlic. Add the tomatoes or tomato paste, okra and three cups of water and boil over low heat for 30 minutes. Okra is very tender and easily broken, so one is careful not to stir them with a spoon, but to shake them in the pan to stir them.

● Fresh beans in tomato sauce ● Peas ● Okra in tomato sauce

Tomatoes garnished with graviera

(Domates me tiri graviera ya garnitoura)

4 servings

8 medium-sized ripe tomatoes

1 small tin evaporated milk

4 tbsps grated graviera

Salt, pepper, pinch sugar

Mint

Fresh butter

W ash tomatoes and cut into thick slices. Arrange in a baking dish. Pour over the undiluted evaporated milk, salt, pepper, mint and sugar. Sprinkle over the grated cheese and dot with butter. Bake in a moderate oven until tomatoes are cooked. Can be used to garnish meat roasted in the oven or on the grill. Serve hot.

Courgette rissoles (Kolokythokeftedes)

10-12 servings

1 kg courgettes

200 gr crumbled feta cheese

1/2 teacup grated kefalotiri

2 potatoes, boiled and mashed

3 eggs

Salt, pepper, mint

3 tbsps toast crumbs

Flour, oil for frying

W ash and cut off ends of courgettes. Grate and salt. Leave for an hour and then squeeze to remove excess liquid. Beat eggs lightly. Put the grated courgettes in a bowl with the cheeses, potatoes, toast crumbs, pepper and 1 tbsp flour. Mix well. Shape the rissoles, flour and fry in hot oil.

Greek-style fresh mushrooms

(Manitaria ala ellinika freska)

4 servings

500 gr fresh mushrooms

12 small onions

250 gr dry white wine

4 tbsps oil

1 tsp dried oregano

Fresh dill

Bayleaf

1 tsp tomato paste

Salt, pepper

I nto a saucepan put the oil, wine and tomato. Place on low heat and stir. Add the cleaned, sliced mushrooms, finely chopped onions, salt, pepper, oregano, bayleaf and dill. Cook for about 30 minutes. Serve hot.

Leeks with wine (Prasa krasata)

4 servings

1 kg leeks

12 small onions

1 glass dry white wine

1/2 teacup oil

1 bayleaf

Salt, pepper

Cayenne pepper (optional)

Cut the leeks and onions into pieces and sauté in the oil. Pour over the wine and then add the sieved tomatoes, bayleaf, salt, pepper (and cayenne pepper if desired) and a little water. Cook for 20-25 minutes.

Fried aubergines with eggs and yoghurt (Melitzanes tiganites me avgo ke yiaourti)

4 servings

2 round medium-sized aubergines

250 gr yoghurt

4 eggs

Salt, pepper

Oil for frying

Wash the aubergines, cut off stems and slice. Heat oil in pan, fry the aubergines and place on absorbent paper. Then fry the eggs. Divide the aubergines between the four plates, and on each put a tbsp of yoghurt and one egg.

Aubergines with tomato and yoghurt
(Melitzanes me domata ke yiaourti)

4 servings

1/2 teacup butter

1/2 teacup oil

1 kg round black aubergines

1 large onion

1 tsp oregano

1 clove garlic

1/2 tsp sugar

250 gr yoghurt

3 tbsps grated cheese

Toast crumbs

Wash aubergines, cut off stems and slice. Heat oil in frying pan and fry aubergines. Put butter in a saucepan and sauté the chopped onion and garlic. Add salt, pepper, sugar, oregano, chopped tomatoes and a little water. Boil for 10 minutes. Stir yoghurt into the sauce. Put the aubergines in a buttered baking dish and pour over the sauce. Sprinkle with the cheese and toast crumbs. Bake in moderate oven for 20-25 minutes until cheese is browned.

Broad beans with oil and oregano

(Koukia me ladorigani)

4 servings

500 gr dried broad beans

3 medium onions, chopped

1 teacup oil

1/2 tsp oregano

Salt, pepper

S oak the beans in water overnight. Next day, remove the black spot from the beans with a knife. Boil in a little water, add the oil, oregano, salt, pepper and cook until all the liquid has been absorbed, the beans are tender and only the oil remains.

Stuffed tomatoes and peppers

(Domates ke piperies gemistes)

6 servings

8 ripe tomatoes

4 large green peppers

1 teacup rice

2 medium onions

1-1/2 teacup oil

1 tin peeled tomatoes

4-5 potatoes

1/2 teacup raisins (or currants)

2 tbsps pine nuts or blanched

  almonds

Parsley

2 tsps salt

Pepper, pinch sugar

W ash tomatoes and slice off top with sharp knife. Hollow out the inside of the tomatoes and add salt and a pinch of sugar to each. Wash peppers, cut open tops and remove seeds. Heat a little oil in a pan and sauté the chopped onions; add the rice and sieved tomatoes. Boil for 5 minutes, adding 1 teacup water. Let boil for about 30 minutes. Remove from heat and add the parsley, pinenuts, raisins, salt and pepper. Fill tomatoes and peppers with this mixture. Cut the peeled potatoes into large pieces. Arrange the tomatoes and peppers in a baking pan and fill in the spaces with the potatoes. Pour over the remaining oil, chopped tomatoes and 2 teacups water. Bake in moderate oven for about 1 hour 30 minutes. Serve hot or cold.

Fresh boiled broad beans with garlic

sauce (Koukia freska vrasta me skordalia)

4 servings

1 kg fresh broad beans

8 cloves garlic

1/2 kg boiled potatoes

1 teacup oil

Salt, pepper, vinegar

C ut the ends off the beans, wash and boil in plenty of salted water. Prepare the garlic sauce as follows: peel the garlic and crush either with mortar and pestle or in a blender. Add potatoes and then the oil bit by bit, the salt, pepper and a little vinegar. Then drain the beans, place on a platter and serve with the garlic sauce.

● **Broad beans with oil and oregano** ● **Stuffed tomatoes and peppers**

6 servings

500 gr dried butter beans

2 medium onions

2 medium carrots

1 stalk celery

1-1/2 cup oil

12 rashers bacon

1 tin peeled tomatoes

1 hot pepper

Salt, pepper

Butter beans from Edessa (Gigantes Edessis)

S oak beans in water overnight. In the morning, drain beans and place in saucepan with fresh water to boil. Peel and chop the onions, carrots and celery and add to pan with the beans. When cooked, cut bacon in small pieces and fry lightly in a frying pan. Add the bacon and sieved tomatoes to the beans. Add salt, pepper and the hot pepper. Turn out into a baking pan, add the oil and bake in moderate oven for about 30 minutes.

6 servings

500 gr butter beans

1-1/2 teacup oil

2 peeled carrots

2 medium onions

1 small tin peeled tomatoes

Celery and basil

Salt, pepper

Baked butter beans in tomato sauce
(Gigantes yachni sto fourno)

S oak the beans in water overnight. Next day boil in plenty of water for 15 minutes and drain. In a large kettle place the water, beans, finely chopped onion, carrots, celery and boil for about one hour. Add the sieved tomatoes, 2-3 fresh basil leaves (or 1 tsp dried basil), the oil, salt and pepper. Place in a baking pan and bake in a moderate oven until most of the liquid has been absorbed.

6-7 servings

600 gr dried butter beans

1 teacup flour

1/2 tsp tomato paste

2 teacups oil

1 teacup mayonnaise

Ketchup

Salt, pepper

Fried butter beans (Gigantes tiganiti)

S oak beans in water overnight. Next day, boil in plenty of water until tender. Drain. Put in a bowl the flour and tomato paste; add salt, pepper and water to make a smooth batter. Heat the oil in a frying pan, dip the beans one by one in the batter and fry. Blend the ketchup and mayonnaise in a bowl, and serve as a sauce with the fried beans.

Mixed baked vegetables (from Macedonia) (Briam Makedonias)

6 servings

6 medium aubergines

4 courgettes

6 tomatoes

2 red peppers

2 green peppers

4 medium onions

Chopped parsley

2 cloves garlic

2 teacups oil   Salt, pepper

Wash and slice the aubergines, courgettes, onions and peppers. Fry the aubergines, spread in a medium baking pan. Add the remaining vegetables, oil, parsley, salt, pepper and chopped tomatoes. Cover with aluminium foil and bake in moderate oven without adding water.

Cabbage with rice from Thrace
(Lahanorizo Thrakis)

4 servings

1 medium cabbage

1 cup oil

1/2 cup rice

1 small tin peeled tomatoes

1 onion

Salt, pepper

Wash and slice the aubergines, courgettes, onions and peppers. Fry the aubergines, spread in a medium baking pan. Add the remaining vegetables, oil, parsley, salt, pepper and chopped tomatoes. Cover with aluminium foil and bake in moderate oven without adding water.

Dried beans in tomato sauce
(Fasolia xera yachni)

6 servings

500 gr dried beans

1 cup oil

3 medium onions

3 carrots

2 tablespoons chopped celery
  leaves

Salt, pepper

1/2 tin peeled tomatoes or
  1 tsp tomato paste

Chopped parsley

Soak beans in water overnight. Boil in plenty of water for about an hour and drain. Prepare sauce as follows: Into a saucepan put the oil, chopped onions, carrots, celery and parsley and sauté until onions are golden. Sieve tomatoes and add to sauce. Cook for half an hour. Then add the beans to the sauce and cook for a few minutes more or until done.

Stewed potatoes (from Cyprus)
[Patates antitinachtes (Kyprou)]

4 servings

750 gr small round potatoes

2 tbsps coriander

1 teacup oil

1 teacup red wine

Salt, pepper

P eel, quarter and wash the potatoes. Place the oil in a saucepan, sauté the potatoes well and add the salt, pepper and coriander. Add the wine, a little water and reduce heat. Simmer for about 20 minutes and remove from heat. Serve with roast meat or chicken.

Artichokes and eggs (Anginares sfoungato)

4 servings

3 artichokes

8 eggs

3/4 teacup oil

Salt, pepper

R emove leaves from artichokes, peel tough skin around stem and remove choke. Slice thinly. Heat oil in frying pan, flour artichoke pieces and sauté lightly. Beat the eggs and add to pan. Reduce heat and cook slowly. Cut the sfoungato in four pieces and turn so as to cook on the other side. Serve hot.

Savoury Cretan egg dish (Sfoungato Kritis)

8-10 servings

250 gr fresh green onions

1/2 teacup butter

1/2 kg minced beef

1/2 kg courgettes

Fresh dill, salt, pepper

2 tbsps toast crumbs

6 eggs

C lean, wash and finely chop onions. Heat oil in frying pan and sauté onions with the sliced courgettes, salt, pepper and a finely chopped sprig of fresh dill. Sauté the minced beef in another pan. In a buttered baking dish which has been sprinkled with the toast crumbs, place first the minced meat and then the onions and courgettes. Break the eggs on top one by one. Bake in moderate oven for a few minutes. Serve hot.

Cauliflower au gratin

(Kounoupidi me tiri sto fourno)

4 servings

1 cauliflower, about 2 kg

2 tbsps vinegar

Salt, pepper

4 tbsps butter

2 teacups grated graviera

Wash cauliflower with water and vinegar and cut into flowerets. Cook cauliflower in boiling, salted water for about 30 minutes. Drain and place in buttered baking dish. Salt, pepper, dot with butter and sprinkle with the grated cheese. Bake in moderate oven for about 10 minutes. Serve hot.

Macedonian-style cauliflower

(Kounoupidi makedoniko)

4 servings

1 medium cauliflower

3 tbsps butter

4 slices ham

1 small tin mushrooms

1 teacup graviera

3 tbsps grated cheese

1 teacup sieved tomatoes

Salt, pepper

Wash and cut cauliflower. Boil in salted water for about 30 minutes. Drain and place in buttered baking dish. Pour over tomato, add mushrooms and cubed cheese and ham. Sprinkle with grated cheese and bake in moderate oven for 15-20 minutes. Serve hot.

poultry

- Roast chicken
  with potatoes
- Chicken with
  square noodles

Roast chicken with potatoes

(Kotopoulo me patates sto fourno)

4-5 servings

1 chicken up to 1-1/2 kg

1-1/2 kg small round potatoes

Juice of 2 lemons

1 teacup oil

1 tbsp mustard

3 cloves garlic

Salt, pepper

Wash chicken. Salt and pepper cavity and rub with mustard. Rub outer skin with the juice of one lemon and place in a roasting pan. Peel and wash potatoes. Place in the pan, sprinkle with a little salt and the juice of one lemon. Add oil and a little water. Roast in moderate oven for a total of about 1-1/2 hour. When golden brown, turn chicken over.

Chicken with square noodles

(Kotopoulo me hilopites)

6 servings

One chicken 1-1/2 kg

1/2 kg square noodles

1/2 teacup oil

1 teacup butter

1 small tin of mushrooms, chopped

5 cups water

Salt, pepper

Cut the chicken into 6 portions. Heat oil and a little butter in a pot, sauté chicken well on all sides. Add the sieved tomato, salt, pepper and a few tbsps water. Cook chicken for about 1 hour. When tender, add mushrooms. In another large pot, cook the noodles in plenty of salted water. When ready (about 30 minutes), drain. Melt the remaining butter and pour over noodles.

Chicken with broccoli (Kotopoulo me brokola)

5-6 servings

One chicken 1-1/2 kg

1 kg broccoli

6 tbsps butter

8 level tbsps flour

2 1/2 teacups cold milk

Salt, pepper

2 eggs, beaten

1/2 teacup grated graviera cheese

Boil the chicken and broccoli separately. Remove meat from bones. Place the boiled broccoli and chicken in a buttered baking dish. Prepare sauce: Melt butter in a saucepan, add flour, stir for a few minutes and add the cold milk. Stir constantly until thick. Remove from heat, add salt, pepper, grated cheese and the two eggs. Mix well and pour over the chicken and broccoli. Bake in moderate oven until brown.

Chicken with mushrooms

(Kotopoulo me manitaria)

5 servings

One chicken 1-1/2 kg

8 tbsps butter

25 small onions

1/2 kg mushrooms

1 bayleaf

Salt, pepper

1/2 glass sweet red wine

1 tin peeled tomatoes

S auté the chicken, onions and mushrooms in butter. Add the bayleaf, salt, pepper and wine. Add the sieved tomato and simmer for about 1 hour or until chicken is tender.

Chicken à la Anna (Kotopoulo "Anna")

6 servings

One chicken 1-1/2 kg

4 tbsps butter

6 slices ham

6 slices graviera cheese

1 cup sweet red wine

1/2 glass brandy

1/2 glass vermouth

Salt, pepper

C ut chicken into 6 portions, wash, salt and pepper. Heat butter and sauté chicken on all sides. Add the brandy and wines. Cover pot and simmer. When chicken is tender, remove from heat and cool. Remove bones and wrap each portion of chicken in a slice of ham to make a package. Place packages in a buttered baking dish. Place a slice of cheese over each package and bake until cheese melts. Serve on platter with the sauce from the chicken.

Chicken with green peppers

(Kotopoulo me prasines piperies)

6 servings

One chicken 1-1/2 lb

1 kg green peppers

100 gr black olives from Kalamata

1/2 cup dry white wine

1 medium onion

1/2 teacup oil

1/2 teacup butter

1 glass water

Salt, pepper

Cut chicken into 6 portions. Wash and cut peppers in large pieces. Heat oil and butter in a pan and sauté onion, chicken and peppers. Add wine and a little water, salt and pepper. Simmer for about 1 hour. Just before serving, add the olives.

Chicken livers with bacon

(Sikotakia poulion me beikon)

6 servings

1/2 kg chicken livers

8 rashers bacon

Oil

Cut bacon into about 3 pieces each. Wash the livers and wrap in bacon pieces. Heat oil in frying pan and fry. Ready when bacon is cooked. Serve hot.

Chicken in tomato sauce

(Kotopoulo kokkinisto)

6 servings

One chicken 1-1/2 kg

1 kg potatoes

2 tbsps butter

1 teacup oil

1 onion

1 tin peeled tomatoes

Salt, pepper

Cut chicken into 6 portions. Heat butter and a little oil in pan. Sauté chicken and chopped onions. Add sieved tomatoes, salt, pepper and a little water. Cook for about 1 hour. When chicken is tender, put remaining oil in frying pan and fry potatoes. Serve hot with chips and pour over sauce.

● Chicken with green peppers ● Chicken livers with bacon

● **Stuffed roast turkey**

8-10 servings

1 turkey, about 5 kg

1/2 kg chestnuts

1 teacup butter

1/2 kg minced meat

1 medium onion

1/2 tsp cinnamon

Salt, pepper

1/4 tsp ground cloves

1/2 cup dry white wine

1/2 teacup sultanas

2 tbsps pinenuts

1/4 teacup rice

Stuffed roast turkey (Galopoula yemisti)

S auté the minced meat, chopped onion and turkey giblets in butter. Add the chestnuts, cinnamon, cloves, salt, pepper, pinenuts, sultanas and wine. Add a little water and the rice and simmer for about 30 minutes. Stuff the turkey and sew up cavity. Bake in a pre-heated oven for 3-4 hours or until tender. Serve on platter garnished with the stuffing.

6 servings

One chicken 1-1/2 kg

1/2 kg rice

1 teacup oil

1/2 teacup butter

1 onion

3 tsps peas

1 tin peeled tomatoes

Salt, pepper

5 teacups water

Chicken with rice (Kotopoulo me rizi)

C ut chicken into 6 portions. Heat butter and oil in a saucepan and sauté chicken and chopped onion. Add sieved tomatoes, salt, pepper and a little water. Cook for about one hour, or until the chicken is tender and the sauce thick. Prepare the rice as follows: Place half the butter in a pan with the rice and sauté lightly. Add 5 cups water, a little salt and pepper and cook over low heat for about 30 minutes.When all the water has been absorbed, remove from heat and add the boiled peas. Put rice into a mould and press down well so it takes the shape. Turn out on a platter and arrange the chicken around it. Pour over sauce.

• Chicken with rice • Chicken in tomato sauce

meat - minced meat

- Moussaka
- White beans with country-style sausages
- Pork chops in wine sauce

6 servings

1 kg aubergines

1/2 kg potatoes   *802.4 c.*

1/2 kg minced meat   *1.1 LBS.*

1 small tin peeled tomatoes

1/3 teacup oil

2 chopped onions

1 bayleaf

1 clove garlic

1-1/2 teacup grated cheese

Oil for frying

Salt, pepper

White sauce

1 teacup butter

1 teacup flour

4 teacups cold milk

2 eggs

Salt, pepper, nutmeg

Moussaka (Mousakas)

Wash and slice aubergines, peel and slice potatoes thinly; fry aubergines and potatoes in the oil. In another pan, sauté the onions and garlic, add the minced meat and sauté well for 10 minutes, stirring constantly. Add the tomatoes, salt and pepper, reduce heat and cook for 30 minutes. Layer half the fried potato slices in a buttered baking pan. Cover with half the minced meat mixture and sprinkle with grated cheese. Layer the remaining potatoes, the aubergines and the other half of the meat mixture. Prepare the white sauce as follows: place the butter in a saucepan to melt, add the flour and stir continuously for five minutes; then add the cold milk little by little, and continue stirring until the sauce boils. Remove the pan from the heat. Add salt, pepper and nutmeg. Beat two eggs, add to sauce and mix well. Pour the white sauce over the moussaka and bake for about 40 minutes or until well browned. Wait at least 15 minutes before cutting. Serve with village salad.

4 servings

500 gr white beans

1 teacup oil

500 gr peeled tomatoes

1 onion, chopped

5 fresh green onions, chopped

Basil, salt, pepper

4 country-style sausages

4 tbsps grated cheese

3-4 cloves garlic

White beans with country-style sausages (Fasolia aspra me horiatika loukanika)

Boil the beans for 30 minutes or until tender. Drain. Sauté the onion; add tomatoes, onions and garlic and let sauce boil for 10 minutes. Add a little basil, salt and pepper to the sauce. Place the boiled beans in a baking dish and pour over the sauce. Add the sausages and sprinkle with grated cheese. Bake in moderate oven for 15-20 minutes.

Country-style pork chops in wine

sauce (Brizoles hirines horiatikes krasates)

4 servings

4 pork chops

1 glass red wine

100 gr feta cheese

4 tbsps butter

Few black olives

Salt, pepper, oregano

Flour

Wash the chops well, salt and pepper them. Sprinkle with oregano and flour. Heat butter in frying pan. Fry chops, adding wine at the end. Place in baking dish, add the (pitted) olives, and place a slice of feta cheese on each chop. Bake in moderate oven for 15-20 minutes. Serve with chips.

Baked meat with tomatoes

(Vodino ala hasapa)

5 servings

1 kg beef

1 kg ripe tomatoes

250 gr kefalotiri

4 tbsps oil or butter

Salt, pepper

Wash meat and cut into slices. Place the slices in a pan, salt and pepper. Cut the cheese in slices and place on top of the meat. Wash and slice the tomatoes and arrange over the cheese. Pour over the oil mixed with a little water, cover pan with aluminium foil and bake in a moderate oven.

Country-style sausages (how to make

them) (Horiatika loukanika)

About 25 sausages

500 gr pork

500 gr bacon

1/2 tsp cinnamon

1/2 tsp nutmeg

1/2 tsp cloves

1/2 tsp allspice

Thyme, pepper corns, salt

5 medium intestines, well washed

Run the meat through the meat grinder and place in a large bowl. Add the bacon, cut in large pieces, spices, salt and pepper and knead well so the mixture is uniform. Fill the intestines with this mixture, binding every 10-12 cm. After the sausages are filled, they are allowed to smoke beside the fireplace, or hang in the sun.

5 servings

1 kg veal shoulder

1/2 teacup oil

3 onions

2 carrots

1 bayleaf

2 cloves garlic

Juice of 2 lemons

1/2 tsp corn flour

Salt, pepper

Veal with lemon sauce (Moschari lemonato)

Cut veal into 5 servings. Wash, place in pan with the butter and oil, sauté lightly and then add lemon juice. Peel the onions and garlic and add to meat. Add two glasses of water, cover and simmer. To make the sauce thicker, you can mix 1/2 tbsp corn flour with a little dry white wine and add it to the sauce, allowing it to cook for a few minutes longer. Serve with mashed potatoes or rice.

5 servings

1 kg veal

1 kg small onions

3 tbsps butter

4 tbsps vinegar

4 chopped tomatoes

4 cloves garlic

2 bayleaves

1 sprig rosemary

　(or 1 tsp dried rosemary)

1 teacup oil

1 stick cinnamon

1 glass dry red wine

Salt, pepper

Veal ragout with onions (Moschari stifado)

Cut the meat into 5 servings, place in pan with butter and sauté. Add wine. Then add salt, pepper, tomatoes, finely chopped garlic, bayleaf, rosemary and cinnamon. Peel onions and place in frying pan with the oil, sauté and add to the meat. Add the vinegar and as much water as necessary for the meat to cook over low heat for about 1 hour and 30 minutes.

4 servings

1 kg calves' liver

1/2 teacup oil

Flour

Salt, pepper

Fried calves' liver (Sikoti moscharisio tiganito)

Cut the liver into thin strips. Salt, pepper and flour. Heat oil in a frying pan and fry the liver. Serve hot with chips.

● Veal with lemon sauce ● Veal ragout with onions

Piquant lambs' or calves' liver
(Sikoti arnisio i moscharisio marinato)

4 servings

1-1/2 kg liver

1/2 teacup oil

2 level tbsps flour

1/2 tin tomatoes, sieved

2 tbsps vinegar

2 bayleaves

2 teacups water

Salt, pepper, rosemary

Cut the liver into small pieces, flour and fry in hot oil. Remove from pan with slotted spoon and keep hot. Mix flour with a little cold water then add to the frying pan. Add vinegar, bayleaves and rosemary and boil for a few moments stirring constantly until the sauce thickens. Finally return the liver to the sauce and cook for a few minutes. Serve hot or cold.

Lamb's liver with rice (Sikoti arnisio pilafi)

4 servings

1 lamb's liver (about 1 kg)

1 teacup rice

1 small tin peeled tomatoes

4 tbsps butter

1 onion, chopped

1 cinnamon stick

1/2 teacup brandy

Salt, pepper

Cut the liver into small pieces. Place half the butter in a pan with the onion and stir with a wooden spoon until golden. Add the liver, cinnamon, salt, pepper and sieved tomatoes. Allow to simmer on low heat. In another pan, cook the rice in 3 cups water with 1 tsp salt and the remaining butter for 20 minutes. Serve liver with rice on a platter.

Veal stew from Epirus
[Moschari lykiotiko (Ipeirou)]

7-10 servings

2-1/2 kg veal

1-1/2 kg onions

1 teacup oil

1/2 teacup butter

1 small tin peeled tomatoes

Salt, pepper

Cut meat into 7-10 servings and wash well. Peel and slice onions, place in pan with 1/2 cup of water and boil on low heat for about 15 minutes. When soft, add the butter and meat and sauté. Then add the oil and sieved tomatoes, salt, pepper and 1 cup of water. Cover pan and simmer meat on low heat for about one hour. Add water as needed. Remove meat onto a platter and serve hot with rice.

Stewed cabbage with sausages
(Lahano yachni me loukanika)

4 servings

8 country-style sausages

1 cabbage

4 tbsps butter

2 onions, chopped

Chopped parsley

1 bayleaf

3 cups water

1 teacup sieved tomatoes

Salt, cayenne pepper

Remove the tough outer leaves of the cabbage and chop coarsely. Sauté onions in a pan with the butter. Then add the tomatoes, bayleaf, salt and pepper and simmer for 15 minutes. Add cabbage. Cover the pan, reduce heat and allow to simmer. When the cabbage is cooked, add the sausages, cook for another 10-15 minutes and then serve.

"Little boat" courgettes
(Kolokythakia varkoules)

4 servings

4 large courgettes

2 medium onions

1 clove garlic

200 gm minced beef

4 tbsps oil

1/2 teacup grated cheese

2 sieved tomatoes

Salt, pepper

Cut the courgettes lengthwise and boil in salted water for 15 minutes. When cool, hollow out with a spoon and arrange in a buttered baking dish. Chop onions and garlic and sauté in oil. Then add the minced meat and stir well for about 10 minutes. Add the tomato, salt and pepper and cook over medium heat for 30 minutes. When the meat is ready, fill the courgettes, then sprinkle with grated cheese, bake for 5-10 minutes and serve.

Meatloaf (home style)
[Kimas sti forma (spitiko)]

6-8 servings

1-1/2 kg minced beef

1 level tsp mustard

1 medium onion, chopped

1 egg

1 clove garlic, finely chopped

1 teacup oil

1 level tbsp flour

1/2 teacup evaporated milk

Cinnamon, salt, pepper

Place all ingredients in a bowl and mix well. Place mixture in buttered loaf pan. Cover pan with aluminium foil and bake in moderate oven. When cooked, allow to cool for about an hour, and then turn it out on a platter slightly larger than the loaf pan. Serve sliced with chips.

Drunkard's titbits (O mezes tou bekri)

4 servings

Liver, heart, lungs, spleen etc.
of one lamb

2 kidneys

150 gr kefalotiri cheese

2 onions, chopped

Juice of 1 lemon

Thyme, oregano

Salt, pepper

1/2 teacup oil

1 glass red wine

B oil water and blanch the liver, heart, lungs and spleen. Chop into small pieces together with the kidneys. Heat oil in pan, and add the meat and onions and stir well. When meat has browned nicely, add the cubed cheese. When done, add wine and lemon juice and finally, the salt, pepper, thyme and oregano and cook for about 30 minutes. Serve hot.

Breaded brains (Myala pane)

4 servings

2 calves' brains

Vinegar, few drops of lemon juice

3 eggs

Toast crumbs

Oil for frying

Salt, pepper

1 whole onion

1 stalk of celery

S oak the brains in cold water with a little vinegar and lemon. Remove the membranes. Heat some water in a pan, add a little vinegar, salt, the celery and the whole, peeled onion. When the water boils, add the brains and boil for about 20 minutes. When cooked, cut into thick slices. Beat the egg well in a soup bowl with a little water. Put the toast crumbs in another bowl. Dip the pieces of brain one by one in the egg first and then in the crumbs. Heat the oil in a frying pan and fry the meat. Serve hot with lemon slices.

Country-style pork chops
(Brizoles hirines horiatikes)

6 servings

6 pork chops

6 tbsps butter

6 cubes feta cheese

Few black olives

Oregano, salt, pepper

T ake a piece of aluminium foil, place a chop in the middle, adding salt, pepper and oregano. On top, place a tbsp of butter, a cube of feta and a few olives, wrap well and place in a baking pan. Do likewise for the remaining chops. Bake in a hot oven for 30-35 minutes. Serve wrapped.

Pork chops in wine sauce

(Brizoles hirines krasates)

4 servings

4 pork chops

2 glasses red wine

1 tsp coriander

Rosemary

1 bayleaf, oregano

4 tbsps butter

Salt, pepper

P lace the chops in a bowl overnight with the salt, pepper, coriander, rosemary, bayleaf, oregano and wine. The next day, drain and fry in butter. Add marinade and cook until meat is tender. Serve hot with chips.

Meat pasties from Thrace

(Tsoubourekia Thrakis)

20 pasties

1 kg flour

1 egg

1 tsp baking powder

1/2 kg minced meat

1 tsp chopped parsley

2 onions, chopped

Salt, pepper, water

Oil for fryimg

M ix flour and baking powder. Add egg and enough water to make a firm dough. Divide dough into 20 pieces, and shape them into balls. Mix the minced meat with the parsley and onion. Add salt and pepper. Roll out the balls of dough one by one, placing a spoonful of the meat mixture on each. Fold over the dough and press edges down with a fork. Heat plenty of oil in a frying pan and fry the pasties. Served hot on a bed of parsley.

Stewed veal from Corfu [Sofrito (Kerkyras)]

4 servings

1/2 kg veal

1 glass dry, red wine

3 cloves garlic

1 tbsp flour

2 tbsps butter

Salt, pepper

C ut meat into 4 servings and pound. Salt, pepper and flour it. Heat butter in frying pan and sauté meat, then remove and place in a saucepan. Put garlic and flour in the frying pan and sauté well, then add to meat together with the wine and a cup of water. Mix well to dissolve the flour, then place saucepan on medium heat and cook until the meat is tender and the sauce is thick. Serve with mashed potatoes.

Sausages and green peppers from Pelion (Spetsofai pilioreitiko)

4 servings

1 kg aubergines

1/2 kg small green peppers

1/2 teacup oil

1 kg peeled tomatoes

1/2 kg country-style sausages

Salt, pepper

Cut the aubergines into thin slices and sprinkle them with salt. Let stand for 30 minutes. Then rinse and drain. Cut the peppers in half, remove seeds and wash. Slice tomatoes and sausages. Heat oil in frying pan and fry the aubergine slices. Remove with slotted spoon. In the same oil fry the peppers and sausages. When they have all been fried, put the aubergines back, adding a little salt and pepper and place all the ingredients in a pan in the oven. Cover the pan with a piece of aluminium foil and bake in a moderate oven for about half an hour.

Fricassee of lamb (Arnaki frikase)

4 servings

1 kg of lamb shoulder

1/2 kg fresh green onions

2 heads of lettuce

1 tsp fresh dill

Juice of 2 lemons

2 eggs

1 tbsp corn flour

2 tbsps butter

1/2 teacup of oil

4 cups water

Salt, pepper

Cut the meat into 4 portions, wash well and sauté lightly in the butter. Meanwhile, wash onions and lettuce and chop. Remove the meat from the pan and place a layer of onions in the bottom of the pan, with the meat next and the lettuce on top. Add salt, pepper and water. Cook until meat is tender. Prepare the egg-and-lemon sauce: beat the eggs with a fork in a bowl, add the lemon juice and a little liquid from the meat. Mix the corn flour with a little cold water and add it to the egg mixture. Pour into the pan with the meat, shaking the pan to blend all the ingredients. Remove pan from heat. Serve hot.

● Fricassee of lamb ● Sausages and peppers (Pelion)

Lambs' trotters with egg and lemon sauce (Podarakia arnisia avgolemono)

6 servings

12 lambs' trotters

2 large onions

2 stalks celery

1 leek

1 bayleaf

6-8 peppercorns

4 level tbsps flour

3 tbsps butter

1 glass milk

2 egg yolks

Juice of 1 lemon

Parsley, salt, pepper

Wash the trotters well, place in boiling water and cook for 10 minutes. Drain, rinse well. Return to pot with plenty of water and let simmer. Add salt, pepper, bayleaf, onions, leek, and celery. Skim off foam from time to time. When the trotters are done, remove from the liquid. Place butter in another pan, and when it has melted add the flour and stir well. Add the cold milk and keep stirring. Add the liquid from the trotters. Beat the egg yolks, add the lemon juice and beat well, then add to the pan which has in the meantime been removed from the heat. Stir well to blend. The soup is served hot with the trotters.

Roast leg of lamb on a spit (Arnisio bouti sti souvla)

6 servings

1 leg of lamb (approx. 2 kg)

4 cloves garlic

Salt, pepper, oregano

Oil

Lemon juice

Wash the meat and with the tip of a knife, make incisions at various points. Peel the garlic and cut in two. Mix salt, pepper and oregano on a plate. Put a piece of garlic and the seasonings in each incision. Season the meat with remaining salt, sprinkle with lemon and a little oil. Put it on the spit in your oven. Turn the oven on and let the spit turn slowly. The meat will need at least two hours to roast.

Lamb with yoghurt (Arnaki me yiaourti)

5 servings

1 kg lamb shoulder

2 onions, chopped

250 gr strained yoghurt

1 level tbsp flour

3 tbsp butter

2 eggs

Juice of 1 lemon

Salt, pepper

Cut the meat into small pieces, salt and pepper. Dredge it in flour. Place butter in pan, then add onion and meat. Sauté until golden brown. Add enough water to cover the meat and boil. When cooked, beat the eggs with the yoghurt and lemon juice, add a little liquid from the meat, and then return the mixture to the pan, removing it from the heat. Serve with rice.

Lamb chops cooked in pastry country style (Paidakia arnisia exohiko)

4 servings

8 lamb chops

8 small potatoes

8 carrots

8 cubes of kefalotiri cheese

2 tbsps peas

250 gr strained yoghurt

2 tsps butter

Salt, pepper

12 sheets of phyllo dough

S alt and pepper the chops and sauté in butter. Sauté the potatoes and carrots briefly in the same butter. Take three sheets of phyllo dough, one on top of the other, buttering each one. On top, place 2 chops, 2 carrots, 2 potatoes, 2 cheese cubes, a few peas and 1 tbsp of yoghurt. Fold the phyllo around the filling to make a square. Place the 4 squares in a buttered baking pan, brush a little butter on top and bake in a moderate oven for 20-25 minutes or until pastry is well browned.

Stuffed spring lamb (Arnaki galaktos gemisto)

8-10 servings

1 spring lamb with offal

200 gr bacon

200 gr butter

2 onions

2-3 bayleaves

5-6 whole allspice

Parsley, rosemary

Mint

3 teacups rice

150 gr pine nuts

200 gr sultana raisins

Salt, pepper

R emove offal (edible organs) from lamb and wash well. Rub lamb with salt, pepper and rosemary and rub cavity with the mint. Prepare stuffing as follows: blanch the offal (liver, heart, spleen, etc.) in boiling water for a few minutes and then remove and chop. Finely chop onion and bacon, place in a saucepan with half the butter and sauté. Sauté the offal in the same pan. Add the rice, boil for just 10 minutes, drain. Put all the ingredients in a bowl: the organs, onions, rice, salt, pepper and butter and mix well. Stuff the lamb with this mixture. Sew the cavity with strong thread. Brush the lamb with oil. Bake lamb for at least 2-1/2 hours in a moderate, pre-heated oven. When cooked, remove the thread and cut the lamb. Serve with the stuffing.

4 servings

Heart, liver, kidney, spleen, and other edible organs from 1 lamb

1 teacup oil

Juice of 2 lemons

1/2 kg lambs' intestines

1 bayleaf

Salt, pepper, oregano

Lambs' offal rolls

(Garthoubes apo sikotaria arniou)

Wash the organs and blanch in boiling water. Clean the intestines and turn them inside out on a thin stick or knitting needle. Wash with plenty of water and salt, and then blanch in boiling water for 1-2 minutes. Place in a bowl and add the salt, pepper, oregano, lemon juice and bayleaf. Cover with a plate and refrigerate. The next day, cut the meat into chunks. Then take a piece each of the liver, lung, spleen, etc. and wrap them up with a piece of intestine. Continue until all the pieces have been used up. Then place the rolls in a pan, pour over the oil and lemon and bake in the oven for about 30 minutes. Serve hot.

8 servings

1 -1/2 kg lamb

1/2 teacup butter

3 onions

2 eggs

Juice of 2 lemons

Fresh dill

Salt, pepper

Stewed lamb with egg and lemon sauce (speciality of Patra)

[Arni aspro yachni (Specialite Patron)]

Cut the meat into 8 servings, wash, salt and pepper. Peel and chop onions finely. Place in pot with the butter, heat. Then add the meat and sauté. Add the dill and 3 glasses of water, leaving the meat to simmer for about 1 hour. When the water has evaporated and just a little sauce remains, remove from heat. Then beat the eggs in a bowl and add the lemon juice, beating constantly. Add a little hot liquid, mix well and pour into the pot. Stir well.

6 servings

1-1/2 kg shoulder or saddle of lamb

1 tin peeled tomatoes

1/2 teacup butter

2 level tsps salt

Pepper

1 tsp sugar

1 cinnamon stick

Lamb stew from Smyrna

(Arni kapama Smyrnis)

Wash meat and cut into portions. Sieve tomatoes. Place meat in saucepan with the tomatoes, salt, pepper, cinnamon and butter. Simmer for about 1-1/2 hour. Before serving, add the sugar and remove cinnamon stick. Serve with rice or mashed potatoes.

Spetses-style braised lamb

(Arnaki kapama ala spetsiota)

6 servings

1-1/2 kg lamb shoulder

Juice of 1 lemon

1/2 cup butter

1 tin tomatoes

1 bayleaf

Salt, pepper

Cut the meat into 6 portions, wash well and sprinkle with lemon juice. Cut tomatoes in half. Place the butter in a saucepan and sauté meat. Add tomatoes, salt, pepper, bayleaf and simmer for about 30 minutes or until the meat is tender and the sauce is thick. Serve with boiled potatoes.

Shoulder of lamb stuffed with spinach (from the Peloponnese)

[Spala arniou gemisti me spanaki (Peloponnisos)]

6-8 servings

1-1/2 kg shoulder of lamb

1/2 kg spinach

3-4 fresh green onions, chopped

Fresh dill

200 gr feta cheese

1 teacup butter

Salt, pepper

Wash the spinach, boil for 4-5 minutes and drain well. Put the butter in a saucepan together with the onions and dill. Add the spinach and sauté. Add the feta, salt, pepper and stir. Spread this stuffing on the shoulder and roll up, tie with string or thread, place in a pan and roast in a moderate oven. When cooked, remove the string and slice. If any juices have remained in the pan, pour over the slices.

Lamb's liver from Roumely

(Sikoti arnisio Roumelis)

6 servings

Liver, kidneys, spleen, heart etc. from 1 lamb

4 onions

5 tbsps butter

1 level tbsp flour

1 glass dry white wine

1 bayleaf

Salt, pepper

3 cloves garlic

1 small tin peeled tomatoes, sieved

Flour

Wash the meat well and cut in chunks. Peel and slice onion and garlic. Flour meat chunks and sauté in butter. Add wine and then the onions, garlic, bayleaf and sieved tomatoes. Simmer for about 30 minutes. When ready, serve with rice.

4-5 servings

1 kg veal

1 carrot

1 medium onion

1 tbsp chopped celery leaves

1/2 teacup butter

2-3 cups water

Salt, pepper

Cold veal (Moschari kryo)

H eat butter in pan, and sauté the meat well, add the carrot, onion, celery, water, salt and pepper. Cover the pan and cook over low heat for 1-2 hours or until tender. Serve cold, sliced.

6 servings

One cabbage, approximately
 1-1/2 kg

1/2 kg minced meat

200 gr rice

2 tbsps flour

2 eggs

Juice of 2 lemons

3 onions, chopped

200 gr butter

Salt, pepper

Chopped parsley

Cabbage rolls with minced meat
(Lahanodolmades me kima)

R emove the outer leaves from the cabbage. Put the cabbage into boiling water for about 15 minutes. Remove, allow to cool and separate the leaves, setting aside the tougher ones, reserving those suitable for wrapping. Sauté the onion with half the butter. Place the minced meat in a bowl, add the rice, parsley, onion, salt and pepper and mix well. Place a little filling on each leaf and wrap. Place a nut of butter on the bottom of the pan, and then spread over a layer of the tougher cabbage leaves. Arrange the rolls on top in circular rows. If any leaves are left, place them on top, add water to cover and the remaining butter. Put a heavy plate on top of the rolls so that they do not move. Cover pan and cook for half an hour. Cabbage rolls can be served with a white sauce.

8 servings

1 kg tripe

3 eggs

1 teacup oil

Toast or rusk crumbs

Salt, pepper

Breaded tripe (Pastsas tiganitos pane)

P repare the tripe and boil in salted water until tender. When it has boiled, cut into pieces. Break 3 eggs into a bowl with 4 tbsps water and beat with a fork. Salt and pepper the tripe and dip the pieces first into the egg and then the crumbs. Heat oil and fry.

● **Cold veal** ● **Cabbage rolls with minced meat**

4 servings

2 spring lambs' heads

2 stalks celery

2 carrots

2 onions

3 teacups water

Salt, pepper

Boiled lambs' heads (Kefalakia arnisia vrasta)

C lean the heads and soak in water for about 30 minutes. Rinse and place in a saucepan with 3 teacups water and boil for about 30 minutes. Peel the onions, carrots and celery and add to pan; then add salt and pepper and cook on low heat for about 15 minutes. When they are done, remove the heads with a slotted spoon. You may add rice to the liquid and make an egg-lemon soup if you wish.

4 servings

4 lambs' brains

6 tbsps butter

Juice of 1 lemon

2 tbsps capers

Vinegar

Salt, pepper

Lambs' brains fried in butter

(Myala arnisia tiganita me voutiro)

W ash brains and place in a pan with cold water, salt and a little vinegar. As soon as the water boils, take pan off heat and remove brains with a slotted spoon. Place the butter in a baking pan, add sliced brains, salt and pepper and bake in a hot oven for 10-15 minutes. A few minutes before taking the brains out of the oven, add the capers.

4 servings

2 calves' brains

3 tbsps vinegar

1 onion, whole

1 celery stalk

3 eggs

Flour

4 tbsps butter

Rusk or toast crumbs

1 tbsp capers

Salt, pepper

Breaded calves' brains

(Myala moscharisia pane)

S oak the brains in a bowl with water and 1 tsp vinegar. Then remove the membranes. Place in a saucepan with cold water and the vinegar, salt, onion and celery. Allow to boil for about 20 minutes. When they have cooled, cut into 8 slices, sprinkle over them salt, pepper and a little flour. Break the eggs into a bowl and beat lightly. Heat the butter in a frying pan. Dip the brain slices first in the egg and then in the rusk or toast crumbs. When they are cooked, remove from frying pan, to which you will then add the remaining butter and the capers, and pour over the brains. Serve with mashed potatoes.

Veal heart ragout with onions

(Carthia moscharisia stifado)

6 servings

1 veal heart

1/2 teacup oil

1-1/2 kg small onions

6-8 cloves garlic

2 peeled tomatoes

2 bayleaves

1/2 cup vinegar

Salt, pepper, pinch sugar

Cut heart in two, wash well and chop. Heat oil in pan, and sauté the pieces of meat. When brown, add vinegar and a little water and cook for a few minutes. Peel the onions and add to the pan together with the peeled, whole garlic cloves, bayleaf, salt and pepper. Sieve and add the tomatoes. Boil for about one hour. If you wish, add a sprig of rosemary and 1/2 cup of dry red wine.

Jellied pig's head (from Macedonia)

(Hirini pichti Makedonias)

8-10 servings

1 pig's head

Juice of 6 lemons

2-3 cloves garlic

1 stalk celery

Salt, peppercorns

Wash head well; place in a pot with water, salt, pepper, garlic and lemon juice. Cook until meat is tender. Remove pan from heat and bone the meat. Cut the meat and tongue into small pieces and place in deep bowls. Strain the liquid and divide among the bowls. Put in a cool place or in the frig until jelled. You may wish to add 1-2 gelatine sheets to speed up the jelling process.

Pork and celery with egg-and-lemon

sauce (Hirino me selino avgolemono)

4 servings

600 gr pork

500 gr celery (1 bunch)

1 tbsp corn flour

3 tbsps butter

1 onion, chopped

2 eggs

Juice of 1 lemon

Salt, pepper

Cut the meat into portions, wash and place in a pan with the onion, butter, salt, pepper and corn flour. Sauté lightly without browning, and add water to cover. Remove strings from celery stalks, cut each stalk into four pieces including some of the leaves and place in pan with the meat. When meat and celery are tender, beat the eggs and add lemon juice. Put in a little liquid from the meat, stirring constantly. Remove pan from heat and pour in the egg-and- lemon mixture. Stir well. Serve hot.

10-12 servings

Liver, heart, kidneys, sweetbreads
and spleen from 1 lamb

Intestines

Oregano, thyme

Salt, pepper

Oil

Juice of 1 lemon

Lambs' offal roast on a spit (Kokoretsi)

Wash the intestines well. Cut up the heart, liver, etc. into medium-sized chunks, wash well and place in a colander to drain. Put in a bowl with the oregano, thyme, salt, pepper and lemon juice. Take a long skewer or spit and spear pieces of the meat from the bowl, one by one. When all pieces have been speared, take the intestines, one by one, spearing them on the end of the spit and wrapping around the meat. Secure ends, then brush with oil and place on the spit in your oven.

6 servings

6 veal chops

1 small tin mushrooms

2 tbsps mustard

Juice of 1 lemon

1/2 tbsp corn flour

1 glass dry, white wine

5 tbsps butter

3 tbsps yoghurt

Salt, pepper

Veal chops with mushrooms and yoghurt
(Brizoles moscharisies me manitaria ke yaourti)

Fry chops in butter and arrange on a platter. Put the sliced mushrooms into the same frying pan, sauté them and add lemon juice and mustard. Mix flour with the wine and add to pan, while stirring with a wooden spoon. Add salt, pepper, yoghurt, always stirring, to make the sauce. Return chops to the pan and heat with the sauce. Serve with mashed potatoes.

4 servings

1/2 kg minced veal

4 cloves garlic

1 tsp grated cumin

1 tin peeled tomatoes

3 tbsps butter

1 cinnamon stick

6 tbsps vinegar

Allspice, salt, pepper

Smyrna sausages (Soutzoukakia smyrnaika)

Place the veal in a bowl with salt, pepper, crushed garlic, cumin and allspice. Mix well, form into sausages and fry in oil. Sieve tomatoes and place in a saucepan with the butter, cinnamon, salt and a pinch of sugar. Let sauce boil and then add the sausages and a little water. Cook for 15-20 minutes. You can also place the sausages in a baking pan, pour over the sauce and bake for 15-20 minutes. Serve with rice or mashed potatoes.

● Lambs' offal roast on a spit ● Veal chops with mushrooms and yoghurt ● Smyrna sausages

4 servings

1/2 kg minced veal

2 rusks

1 onion 1 tbsp grated cheese

4 slices of graviera cheese

1 egg

Oregano, chopped parsley

Salt, pepper

Grilled meat patties with cheese
(Biftekia scharas me tiri)

Put the minced meat in a bowl and grate the onion over it. Add the grated rusks, salt, pepper, grated cheese, parsley, egg and a dash of oregano and mix well. Shape 4 patties and grill them. When done, place a slice of graviera cheese on top and grill until cheese melts. Serve with chips and salad.

6 servings

1-1/2 kg veal

1/2 kg carrots

4 whole onions

2 cloves garlic

1 tomato

1 tsp thyme

1 bayleaf

200 gr green olives

1 glass dry white wine

4 tbsps oil

Salt, pepper

Veal pot roast with olives and carrots
(Psito moschari me elies ke karota)

Heat oil and sauté meat on all sides. Remove meat and put aside. In the same pot, put the whole onions and garlic and sauté. Dice carrots and add to pot together with the chopped tomatoes. Return the meat to the pot and add the wine, salt, pepper, thyme and bayleaf. Cover the pot and simmer for about one hour. Add the olives and let cook for another 15 minutes. Slice meat and garnish with the olives.

4 servings

500 gr minced veal

1 onion

2 rusks

3 tbsps grated cheese

1 tsp finely chopped parsley

16 rashers of bacon

Salt, pepper, oregano

2 tbsps vinegar

Meat patties with bacon
(Souvlaki apo kima ke beikon)

Grate the onion, place in a bowl with the veal, salt, pepper, oregano, parsley and grated rusks and mix well. Shape 16 long narrow patties. Wrap a rasher of bacon around each patty, securing with a toothpick. Place the patties in a baking pan, pour over oil and bake for 10-12 minutes in a hot oven. Serve with chips.

● **Meat patties with cheese** ● **Veal pot roast with olives and carrots**

Meat patties with fried eggs
(Biftekia me avga tiganita)

4 servings

500 gr minced veal

1 medium onion, finely chopped

1 tsp mustard

1 tbsp grated cheese

1 tsp vinegar

2 rusks, soaked in water

4 eggs

3 tbsps oil

Salt, pepper, oregano

P lace all ingredients in a bowl and mix well. Shape 4 large meat patties, pre-heat grill, brush with oil and grill. If you wish, you can also fry them. When they are cooked, fry four eggs in the oil and place on patties. Serve with mashed potatoes or chips.

Calves' liver with onions
(Sikoti moscharisio me kremmidia)

4 servings

1 kg calves' liver

1 kg onions

2 teacups olive oil

1 clove garlic

4 tomatoes, peeled, sieved

Salt, pepper

C ut liver into thin slices. Peel and slice onions. Place in a saucepan 1 teacup of oil, crushed garlic, onions and 2 tbsps water and boil. Heat the remaining oil in a frying pan; salt, pepper and flour liver and fry in the oil. When the liver is done, add it to the onions together with the tomatoes and let boil on low heat for 15-20 minutes.

Veal kidneys flambé
(Nefra moscharisia flambe)

4 servings

500 gr veal kidneys

3 tbsps butter

1/2 cup brandy

1 onion, grated

1 glass dry, white wine

1/2 teacup evaporated milk or

   cream

1/4 tsp curry powder

Mustard, salt, pepper

H eat butter in frying pan. Cut kidneys into chunks, salt and pepper and fry in the hot butter, then add brandy. Remove with a slotted spoon and keep hot. Put the grated onion into the frying pan and fry; then add the curry powder stirrring lightly. Add wine and mustard. Boil sauce for about 15 minutes and when it is thick, add the milk or cream and the kidneys. Serve with mashed potatoes.

● **Meat patties with fried eggs** ● **Calves' liver with onions**

Baked minced meat and potatoes (from Cyprus)

[Pastitsio pafitiko me patates (Kyprou)]

10-12 servings

1 kg potatoes

500 gr minced veal

1 medium onion

1 teacup grated Haloumi (Cypriot cheese)

4 ripe tomatoes

3 tbsps butter

Salt, pepper

1 egg

Wash the potatoes and boil in their skins. Chop onion and place in a saucepan with the butter, meat, salt and pepper and sauté. Add the sieved tomato. Simmer for 30 min. When the potatoes are cooked, peel and mash them. Place the mashed potatoes in a large bowl with the grated cheese and a little salt. Divide into two equal portions. Take a medium-sized baking pan, butter it and spread half the potatoes on the bottom. Put the meat mixture on top, and then the rest of the potatoes. Brush a beaten egg on top. Bake in moderate oven for 10-15 minutes until browned.

Stuffed spleen (Splina yemisti)

4 servings

1 large veal spleen

150 gr grated feta cheese

2 tbsps rusk or toast crumbs

1 tbsp finely chopped parsley

2 cloves garlic finely chopped

1 teacup oil

1 small tin peeled tomatoes

Salt, pepper, oregano

Wash spleen well and cut a pocket lengthwise with a sharp knife. Place next 4 ingredients in a bowl and mix well, adding 1 tbsp oil. Stuff spleen with this mixture and sew up with heavy thread. Sieve tomatoes, put in a saucepan with the remaining oil and add the spleen. Cook for about 1-1/2 hours on low heat. When it is done, remove thread and slice spleen. Pour over sauce.

4-5 servings

1 large veal spleen

1/2 teacup oil

1/2 teacup white wine

8 small onions

1 bayleaf

1 large tomato, chopped

3 cloves garlic

Salt, pepper

Spleen with wine sauce (Splina me krasi)

Remove membrane covering spleen. Cut spleen into narrow strips. Heat oil in pan, add spleen and sauté for 5-6 minutes. Add wine. Peel onions and garlic and add to pan with bayleaf and tomato. Add salt and pepper and cook over low heat for about 30 minutes. Add water if necessary. Serve when all the water has been absorbed and spleen is tender.

fish -
seafood

- Boiled fish with egg
  and lemon soup

Boiled fish with egg and lemon soup

(Psari vrasto me soupa avgolemono)

6 servings

1-1/2 kg fish suitable for boiling

(bass, haddock, seabream)

2 medium onions, chopped

1 stalk celery, 1 potato, 1 carrot

Juice of 2 lemons

1 bayleaf

1/4 cup of oil

8 teacups of water

3 tbsps rice

1 tsp corn flour

2 eggs, salt, pepper

Clean and wash fish well and cut into portions. Sauté lightly the onions, celery, bayleaf, salt, pepper and the juice of 1 lemon in the oil. Add the fish and water. Let boil at low heat about 30 minutes. Then remove the fish. Add the rice to the soup and when it is cooked, make the egg-and-lemon as follows: Beat the eggs well in a separate bowl, add the juice of 1 lemon and corn flour, beating well. Then add this mixture to the soup, removing from the heat immediately. Serve the soup first and then the fish, with oil and lemon, garnished with the vegetables.

Fish soup (Psarosoupa)

6 servings

1-1/2 kg fish suitable for boiling

2 medium onions

2 large potatoes

2 carrots

2 bayleaves,

1 stalk of celery

2 egg yolks

Salt, pepper corns

5 tbsps rice

4 tbsps oil

2 tbsps white wine

2 lemons, 2 tomatoes

7 teacups water

Fill a large kettle with 7 cups of water. Add the carrots, celery, onions, potatoes, pepper corns and salt. Boil for 15 minutes. Wash and clean the fish. Put it in heavy pot and boil for 15-20 minutes. When fish is cooked, remove with a slotted spoon onto a platter. Strain the soup through a colander into a clean pot. Bring soup to the boil and add rice. Boil for about 20 minutes. Whiz vegetables in the blender and then add to soup. Prepare the egg-and-lemon: beat the eggs lightly and add the lemon juice; while still beating, add several spoonfuls of the hot soup and stir. Pour the egg-and-lemon into the soup, stir vigorously and remove from heat. Serve hot, accompanied by the boiled fish garnished with mayonnaise.

Grilled lobster (Astakos scharas)

6 servings

3 lobsters (about 700-800 gr each)

Juice of one lemon

Salt, pepper

Ask your fishmonger to cut the lobsters in two lengthwise, if you cannot do it yourself. Wash them well, turn the grill on, salt and pepper the lobsters on the meat side and place on the grill. The shell should be touching the grill, otherwise the lobster will spill out. After cooking 20-25 minutes on one side so that the meat becomes firm, then turn over and bake on the other side for another 20-25 minutes. On each plate serve half a lobster, a pat of fresh butter and half a lemon.

Baked lobster (Astakos sto fourno)

2 servings

1 lobster (about 1 kg)

4 tbsps butter

1/2 cup brandy

1 cup dry, white wine

3 tbsps undiluted evaporated milk

1 tbsp corn flour

1 tsp mustard

Salt, pepper

Boil lobster in water and vinegar. When cold, cut lengthwise with a knife, and remove meat without breaking the shell. Chop meat. Heat butter in frying pan, sauté lobster, and add brandy. Remove lobster. Mix corn flour with wine and add to frying pan. Stir the sauce well with a spoon, add salt, pepper, mustard and milk. Add the lobster pieces to sauce and fill the shell. Sprinkle grated cheese on top and place in the oven to brown. Serve hot.

Cuttlefish with rice (Soupies me rizi)

4 servings

1 kg cuttlefish

3 onions

1 cup oil

2 teacups rice

1 lemon

Salt, pepper

Clean cuttlefish, as usual, and place in colander to drain. Cut onions in thin slices. Place oil in pan and sauté onions. Add the cuttlefish together with a glass of water and allow to boil. When cooked, add 4 teacups of water, the rice, salt, pepper and lemon juice. Cover pan and lower heat to simmer for 20-25 minutes.

Cuttlefish in tomato and wine sauce
(Soupies me domatakia ke krasi)

4 servings

1 kg cuttlefish

1 teacup oil

1 teacup flour

1/2 cup white wine

2 tbsps chopped parsley

1 teacup tomato juice

2 medium onions, chopped

1 bayleaf, salt, pepper

C lean and wash cuttlefish. Place half the oil in a frying pan; dredge cuttlefish in the flour, and when the oil is hot, fry until golden. Remove. Sauté the onions in the remaining oil, and then add the wine. Add the parsley, tomato juice, bayleaf, salt and pepper and simmer. When the sauce is thick, add the cuttlefish and allow to cook for 15-20 minutes more. Serve hot.

Cuttlefish with spinach (Soupies me spanaki)

4 servings

1 kg cuttlefish

3 large onions

1 kg spinach

1 teacup oil

Juice of one lemon

1 tbsp fresh dill

Parsley, finely chopped

Salt, pepper

W ash the cuttlefish, chop and place in colander to drain. Peel and slice onions, and sauté in the oil until golden. Add cuttlefish and simmer until only the oil is left. Meanwhile, wash and chop the spinach. Put the spinach in pan together with the cuttlefish, dill, parsley, salt and pepper. Cover pan and cook over low heat for about one hour.

Dorado with fresh fennel
(Lithrinia me maratho)

4 servings

4 large dorado

1/2 teacup oil

6 tbsps flour

4 peeled tomatoes

4 tbsps fresh fennel or dill,

  finely chopped

1 bayleaf

Oregano

2 cloves garlic

Chopped parsley

Salt, pepper, pinch of allspice

C lean dorado and remove scales. Wash well, salt and pepper. Sprinkle with lemon juice and dredge in flour. Heat oil in frying pan and fry fish on both sides. When done, remove to a baking pan. Sieve tomatoes and place in a bowl with the fennel, oregano, bayleaf, allspice, garlic and parsley. Blend lightly and cover the fish with this sauce. Bake in moderate oven for 15-20 minutes.

● Cuttlefish in tomato and wine sauce ● Dorado with fresh fennel

Dorado with wine (Lithrinia me krasi)

4 servings

4 average-sized dorado

2 large onions

Sprig of chopped parsley

Pinch of thyme

1 bayleaf

5 ripe peeled tomatoes

4 tbsps butter

Juice of 1 lemon

1/2 kg. dry, white wine

Salt, pepper

C lean the dorado, wash well and arrange in a baking pan. Salt, pepper and sprinkle with lemon juice. Slice onions and place beside the fish together with the garlic and coarsely chopped tomatoes; then add the wine. Cover with aluminium foil. Bake for 25-30 minutes. When cooked, place on platter and sprinkle with fresh parsley.

Tomatoes stuffed with shrimps
(Domates yemistes me garides)

6 servings

6 medium tomatoes

6 tbsps mayonnaise

250 gr shrimps

2 hard-boiled eggs

1 tbsp vinegar

Salt, pepper

W ash tomatoes and cut a thin slice off the top. Remove pulp with a spoon; salt. Wash shrimp. Place a little water and vinegar in a saucepan and when liquid boils, add shrimp. When they have boiled 12-20 minutes, clean them and cut in half. Place the mayonnaise in a bowl with the shrimp, blend well and fill tomatoes with this mixture. Peel and slice eggs. Place one slice on each tomato. If you prefer, reserve 6 whole shrimps and use them as garnish instead of the egg slices.

Eel in tomato sauce (Heli me saltsa domatas)

5 servings

1 kg eel

1 cup oil

3 chopped onions

1/2 cup dry white wine

1 small tin tomatoes

1 bayleaf

Parsley

Salt, pepper

P eel the eel and remove head. Cut into pieces. Place the oil, onion and bayleaf in a pan and sauté lightly. Then add sieved tomatoes, salt and pepper and simmer over low heat. When sauce is thick, add the eel, wine and parsley, cover the pan and cook for about 30 minutes.

Chub mackerel (Smyrna style)
(Kolii smyrnaiiki)

6 servings

1 kg chub mackerel

1 cup oil

Juice of one lemon

1 teacup sieved tomatoes

Flour   1 bayleaf

1 tsp oregano

Sprig rosemary

2 cloves garlic, crushed

1 teacup dry white wine

Salt, pepper, pinch allspice

Cut heads off fish, clean them well and wash. Heat oil in frying pan, dredge fish in flour and fry. Place them in a baking pan, add the salt, pepper, wine, tomato, garlic, bayleaf, rosemary and allspice. Bake for about 30 minutes.

Chub mackerel cooked in wine
(Kolii krasatoi)

6 servings

1 kg chub mackerel

1 medium onion

2 medium carrots

Juice of 1 lemon

Chopped parsley

3 cloves garlic

2-3 cloves

5 tbsps oil

2 cups dry, white wine

1 tsp vinegar

Salt, pepper, pinch oregano

Clean and wash fish well. Chop onions, carrots and garlic. Salt and pepper fish well and place in a baking pan. Pour over the oil, add the oregano, parsley and cloves. Add the onions, garlic, carrots and wine. Bake in moderate oven for about 40 minutes.

Small fish Corfu style
[Gavros ala Korfou (bourtheto)]

4 servings

1 kg small fish

1 cup oil

Juice of two lemons

6 cloves garlic, chopped

1 level tbsp oregano

Clean the fish and remove heads. Wash well, and drain in colander. Place in baking pan, add lemon juice, garlic, oregano, salt, pepper and oil and bake in moderate oven for about 20-25 minutes.

Tinned mussels with rice

(Pilafi me mydia konservas)

6 persons

1 tin mussels

2 teacups rice

1 small tin peeled tomatoes

1 bayleaf

1 chopped onion

1 small glass oil

Salt, pepper

Place the oil and onion in a pan and sauté. Drain the mussels, reserving the liquid. Add the mussels to the onion and sauté lightly. Add sieved tomatoes and cook for a few minutes. Then measure the reserved liquid. There should be 5 teacups; add water to make up the required amount. Add salt, pepper and bayleaf. As soon as the mixture boils, add the rice, stir, cover the pan and simmer for 25 minutes.

Tinned squid with rice

(Rizi pilafi me kalamarakia konservas)

6 servings

1 tin squid

2 teacups rice

1 bayleaf, salt, pepper

1 wineglass oil

This pilaf is made in the same way as the pilaf with mussels, the only difference being that one must remove the transparent bone and chop the squid.

Tagliatelle with seafood

(Taliateles me thalassina)

4-5 servings

1/2 teacup of oil

1 medium onion

1/2 kg tagliatelle

1 clove garlic

1 carrot

1/2 stalk celery

Sprig parsley

1 large tin peeled tomatoes

1/2 teacup dry, white wine

1 tin mussels, 1 tin oysters

1 tin shrimps

Chop onion, garlic, carrot, celery and parsley. Heat the oil and sauté vegetables. Sieve tomatoes, add to vegetables together with the wine. Boil about half an hour for the sauce to thicken. Drain the seafood, add it to the sauce and boil for another 10 minutes. Boil the tagliatelle in plenty of salted water, drain and place on platter. Pour over sauce. Serve hot.

● **Tinned mussels with rice**

Boiled shrimps with oil and lemon
(Garides vrastes ladolemono)

4 servings

1-1/2 kg shrimps

2 tbsps vinegar

Juice of 1/2 lemon

1/2 teacup oil

1 bayleaf

1/2 tsp sweet mustard

Salt, pepper, parsley

Wash shrimp. Place in a pan 1/2 cup water, vinegar and bayleaf. When the water boils, add shrimp and cook for 20-25 minutes. Rinse and clean. Place in a serving dish. Put the mustard, salt, pepper, lemon juice and chopped parsley in a bowl and beat with a fork until well mixed. Pour this sauce over shrimp.

Octopus with wine (Ktapodi krasato)

6 servings

2 kg octopus

2 teacups dry red wine

1 teacup oil

1 bayleaf

Pepper

A few lettuce leaves

Clean and wash octopus and place in a saucepan. Add wine, oil, pepper and bayleaf. Place the saucepan on low heat and allow to cook for about one hour. When the octopus is tender, cool and cut in small pieces. Serve on a platter, on the lettuce leaves.

Octopus with elbow macaroni
(Ktapodi me kofto makaronaki)

6 servings

1 kg octopus

1/2 kg elbow macaroni

1 small tin tomatoes

1/2 cup olive oil

3 chopped onions

1 cinnamon stick

2 glasses water

Salt, pepper

Clean and wash the octopus. Place in saucepan without water on low heat and boil. Discard the water from the octopus and cut meat into small pieces. Put octopus back in the pan with the chopped onion and oil and sauté. Then add sieved tomatoes, salt, pepper and cinnamon. When the octopus is tender, add 5 cups water and the macaroni. Allow to cook for 25-30 minutes.

● **Boiled shrimps with oil and lemon** ● **Octopus with wine**

Fried fish steaks with garlic sauce
(Galeos tiganitos me skordalia)

6 servings

1 kg fish steaks

6 tbsps flour

3 tbsps vinegar

2 lemons

Oil for frying

Pinch salt

Wash and drain fish. Salt lightly, sprinkle with lemon juice and dredge in the flour. Heat oil in frying pan and fry fish. It should be golden brown on both sides. Serve with garlic sauce (see page 26).

Stuffed squid (Kalamarakia gemista)

6 servings

1 kg squid

1-1/2 teacup chopped onion

1 teacup rice

3 tbsps chopped parsley

1 teacup oil

3 tbsps pine nuts

1 cup dry red wine

Salt, pepper

Clean squid by removing transparent bone and wash. Cut tentacles into small pieces, reserving hollow bodies whole. Sauté the onion, tentacles, pine nuts and rice in the oil. Then add wine, parsley, salt and pepper and stir well. The filling is ready. Stuff hollow bodies with the filling, close with toothpick and stand them up in a saucepan. Put in a little water, cover pan and place on low heat. Allow to cook for about 45 minutes. Serve hot or cold.

Squid (from Thessaloniki)
(Kalamarakia Thessalonikis)

6 servings

1 kg squid

4 green peppers

1 tin tomatoes

3 cloves garlic

2 medium onions

1/2 teacup oil

1 tsp dried rosemary

Salt, pepper

Clean squid by removing transparent bone, wash, cut into pieces and drain well. Peel onions and slice; wash and slice peppers. Chop garlic. Heat oil in a frying pan, sauté onions lightly and then add garlic, peppers and squid. Sieve the tomatoes and add them together with the rosemary to the pan. Allow to cook over low heat for 30-35 minutes.

• Fried fish steaks with garlic sauce   • Stuffed squid

Fresh small fish with oil and oregano

(Gavros ladorigani)

4 servings

1 kg fresh small fish

1 cup water

Oregano

1/2 cup oil

Juice of 1 lemon

C lean the fish and remove heads. Wash and drain. Heat water and oil in a saucepan and when the mixture boils, add the fish, lemon juice, oregano, salt and pepper. Allow to cook over low heat for about 20 minutes.

Fresh small fish with tomato (plaki)

[Gavros me domata (plaki)]

4 servings

1 kg fresh small fish

2 medium onions, chopped

1 sprig parsley, chopped

1 small tin tomatoes

1/2 teacup oil

Juice of 1/2 lemon

2 cloves garlic

1 bayleaf, salt, pepper

W ash and clean fish, removing heads. Place in a baking pan, salt, pepper and sprinkle with lemon juice. Sauté onions, garlic and parsley in oil and add sieved tomatoes. Cover fish with the sauce, and bake in moderate oven for 20-25 minutes.

Fried red mullet in piquant sauce

(Barbounia marinata)

4 servings

1 kg red mullet

2 bayleaves

2 cloves garlic

Sprig rosemary

1/2 teacup vinegar

Salt, pepper, flour

1 tsp corn flour

1-1/2 teacup oil

C lean and wash fish; salt, pepper and dredge in flour. Heat oil and fry fish on both sides. Remove fish and add chopped garlic, rosemary and bayleaf to the same oil. Replace the fried fish and add vinegar. If the sauce is too thin, mix the corn flour with a little water or wine, add it to the sauce and allow to cook a few minutes more. (Other fish suitable for cooking in this way are: bogue, saddled bream, sardines, and dorado.)

● Small fish with oil and oregano ● Red mullet in piquant sauce

Red mullet in tomato sauce

(Barbounia me saltsa domata)

4 servings

4 large red mullet

2 teacups oil

2 medium onions, chopped

1 clove garlic

1 tin peeled tomatoes

Sprig rosemary

Salt, pepper

Clean fish, remove scales and wash well. Place side by side in a baking pan and prepare the sauce. Place oil, onion, garlic and rosemary in a saucepan and sauté until onion is golden. Add sieved tomato, salt and pepper. Let the sauce boil 15 or 20 minutes, then pour over the fish. Meanwhile, pre-heat the oven to 180°C and bake mullet for about 30 minutes. Serve with the sauce.

Red mullet in foil (Barbounia sto harti)

4 servings

4 large red mullet

2 pieces butter

Juice of 2 lemons

4 pieces aluminium foil

Salt, pepper

Clean fish, removing scales. Heat oven to 180°C. Pour the lemon juice over fish; salt and pepper each one, rub with butter and wrap carefully in foil. Place in baking pan and bake for 20-25 minutes. Serve fish in foil.

Baked whole fish (Psari olokliro sto fourno)

4 servings

1 fish (bream or sea perch), 1 kg

1 chopped onion

Chopped parsley

1/2 tin peeled tomatoes, sieved

Rosemary

1 bayleaf

2 glasses dry white wine

1 teacup oil

1 clove garlic, chopped

Juice of 2 lemons

Salt, pepper

Clean fish and wash well. Salt, pepper and place in baking pan. Pour over lemon juice. Place on it the chopped onion, garlic, parsley, rosemary and bayleaf. Pour over the wine, oil and tomato. Bake in a pre-heated (150°C) oven for about half an hour. When done, remove the fish whole to a long platter and pour over the sauce.

● Baked whole fish

Tunny fish with piquant sauce
(Psari mayiatiko marinato)

6 servings

6 slices tunny fish

1/2 teacup oil

1 teacup flour

2 onions, sliced

2 cloves garlic, finely chopped

6 tbsps vinegar

2 tsps sugar

Sprig rosemary

Salt, pepper

Wash the fish slices, salt and pepper them. Dredge fish in flour, heat oil in frying pan and fry on both sides. Place fish on platter. Add the onions and garlic to the oil in the frying pan and sauté. Then add sugar, vinegar and rosemary. Cook the sauce for a few minutes and pour over fish. This dish is tastier when served after 4-5 hours.

Fried sole (Glosses tiganites)

2 servings

2 medium sole (about 400 gr.)

1/2 teacup milk

Juice of 2 lemons

Flour for dredging

Oil for frying

Salt, pepper

Remove skin from both sides of fish. Wash well and place fish in a bowl; salt and pepper them, add lemon juice and milk. Refrigerate for at least one hour. Heat oil in frying pan. Dredge fish in flour. Place in the hot oil and fry on both sides. When both fish have been fried, serve with boiled green vegetables or beetroots.

Shrimps baked with cheese
(Garides youvetsakia)

5 servings

1 kg shrimps

1/2 teacup oil

1 small tin peeled tomatoes

1/2 cup of brandy

200 gr. feta cheese

Oregano, thyme

Salt, pepper

Boil and clean shrimp. Place in a frying pan the oil, shrimp, salt, pepper, oregano and thyme, fry for a few minutes then add brandy. Sieve tomatoes and add. Boil just until tomatoes are cooked. Divide the shrimp among 5 individual baking dishes and place a slice of feta on each one. Place the baking dishes in a moderate oven for 10-15 minutes, until the cheese melts.

● **Tunny fish with piquant sauce** ● **Fried sole**

Cod with onions (local dish from Calamata)

[Bakaliaros me kremmidia (topico faghito Kalamatas)]

8 servings

1-1/2 kg salt cod

1 kg onions

1 tin peeled tomatoes

1-1/2 teacup oil

Salt, pepper, flour

S oak cod in water overnight to remove salt. The next day, remove skin and bones, wash well and cut into pieces. Place oil in pan to heat, dredge cod in flour and fry in hot oil. When cod is cooked, remove and sauté onions in the same oil. Then place the oil and onions in a saucepan, add the sieved tomatoes, and a little salt and pepper. Boil for about 15 minutes. Then add the pieces of cod to the sauce. Add water if necessary, and simmer for about 30 minutes, until only the oil is left.

Seabass from Mesolonghi

(Lavraki Mesolonghiou)

4-5 servings

1-1/2 kg seabass

1-1/2 teacup oil

4 tbsps flour

3 tbsps chopped cucumber pickles

3 tbsps capers

2 tbsps chopped parsley

1 small tin peeled tomatoes

Juice of 1 lemon

Salt, pepper

C lean fish, wash well and cut into 5 servings. Place fish in a bowl, sprinkle with the lemon juice, salt and pepper. Place half the oil in frying pan to heat, dredge the fish in flour and fry. After frying, remove fish from pan and add the pickles, capers, parsley and sieved tomato to the same oil. Cook for 5-10 minutes. Place the fried fish in a baking pan and pour over the sauce. Sprinkle with grated cheese (if desired) and bake in moderate oven for 15-20 minutes.

game

- Thrushes in tomato sauce with rice
- Goose with okra
- Rabbit stew with onions

Thrushes in tomato sauce with rice

(Tsicles kokkinistes me rizi)

4 servings

8 thrushes

2 finely chopped onions

1 teacup of butter

1/4 cup dry white wine

1 teacup of rice

1/2 tin of peeled tomatoes

Salt, pepper

Wash the thrushes well and place them in a colander to drain. Then brown the butter well, add the thrushes and brown them on all sides. Add the wine, sieve the tomatoes and add them too. Simmer until birds are tender. Place on a platter. Measure 2 1/2 cups of liquid; if there is not enough, make up the amount with water. Then add the rice, stir lightly, turn the heat down and cook for 15-20 minutes. When the rice is cooked, add the thrushes.

Goose with okra (Hina me bamies)

6 servings

One small (1-1/2 kg) goose

1 kg okra

1 tin of peeled tomatoes

6 tbsps butter

2 finely chopped onions

1 cup of dry white wine

Salt, pepper

Wash and cut the goose into six servings. Place the butter in a pan and sauté the goose. Add the finely chopped onion and sauté. Fill with enough water to cover the goose and let simmer at low heat for about 30 minutes. Add the tomato and let boil for a few minutes. Then add the salt, pepper, okra and wine and simmer until goose is tender. Serve goose and okra on platter and cover with the sauce.

Rabbit stew with onions (Kouneli stifado)

6 servings

One rabbit (1 - 1/2 kg)

1 kg onions (small)

3 tbsps butter

1 cup of sweet red wine

4 tbsps of evaporated milk

Salt, pepper

Wash the rabbit and cut it into six servings. Sauté the rabbit lightly in the butter. Peel onions; add them to top, together with salt, pepper and two cups of water. Cover pot and simmer. When meat is tender, remove the rabbit and onions. Add the wine and milk to the pot. Let the sauce thicken for a few minutes. Serve the rabbit and onions on a platter and pour over the sauce.

Turtle-doves in tomato sauce

(Trygonia kokkinista)

4 servings

4 turtle-doves

4 tbsps butter

1-1/2 cup dry white wine

4 fresh, ripe tomatoes

Salt, pepper

Wash the birds well. Place in pot with the butter, sauté on all sides, and then add the wine and sieved tomatoes. Salt and pepper, and allow the birds to simmer for 25-30 minutes. Serve with mashed or fried potatoes.

Rabbit from Hania, Crete

(Kouneli Hanion Kritis)

4 servings

1 rabbit (about 1-1/2 kg.)

2 onions finely chopped

2 cups of dry white wine

4 tbsps of butter

2 cloves garlic

Sprig of finely chopped parsley

1 bayleaf

Pinch cinnamon, oregano

Salt, pepper

Wash and cut the rabbit and leave to drain for a while. Place the butter in a pot, salt and pepper the rabbit and brown it. Chop the onions, add to the pot with a little water. Simmer until very little sauce remains, then serve with rice or mashed potatoes.

Rabbit with lemon from Crete

(Kouneli lemonato Kritis)

6 servings

1 rabbit (about 1-1/2 kg.)

4 tbsps butter

2 lemons

4 onions

Thyme

1 bayleaf

1 bunch of parsley

4 tbsps undiluted evaporated milk

1 tsp of corn flour

Salt, pepper

Wash rabbit well; cut into 6 servings. Salt and pepper it. Place the butter in a pot, add the rabbit and brown on all sides. Peel the onions, slice and sauté in the same pot. Add the thyme, bayleaf, one lemon peel, the juice of 2 lemons and a little water. Cover the pot and let simmer. When the rabbit is done, remove from pot. Mix the corn flour in a small bowl with one tsp butter, add the milk, and then add all together to the pot in which the rabbit was cooked; allow sauce to cook until thickened. Prepare rice and serve with rabbit.

Rabbit with peppers (Kouneli me piperies)

6 servings

1 rabbit (1-1/2 kg approximately)

1 small tin peeled tomatoes

100 gr black olives

2 cloves garlic

Salt, pepper, pinch basil

1 cup dry, white wine

2 medium onions

1/2 cup butter

1/2 cup oil

5 green peppers

Cut the rabbit into portions, wash well, salt and pepper. Place butter and oil in a pan and sauté the rabbit pieces. Peel and chop onions and garlic, and sauté them in the same pan. Then add the wine. Cut the peppers in half, remove seeds, cut peppers into strips, wash and put them in the pan. Sieve tomatoes and add them, together with the basil and a little water, to the pan. Cover pan, turn down the heat and simmer. When the rabbit is tender, add the olives and cook for about 10 minutes more, then serve.

Duck with peas (Papia me araka)

4-6 servings

1 duck (about 1-1/2 kg)

150 gr bacon

4 large onions

6 tbsps butter

1 kg shelled peas

Oregano, salt, pepper

1 lettuce

Clean and wash the duck. Peel and chop onions finely; cut bacon into pieces. Place butter in pot, add onions and bacon and sauté. Remove and reserve. Salt and pepper the duck, place in pot and brown. Then add the peas and lettuce leaves, bacon, a cup of water and oregano. Cover pot and simmer. When cooked, cut duck into servings and garnish with peas.

Turtle-doves with rice (Trygonia me rizi pilafi)

4 servings

4 turtle-doves

4 tbsps butter

1/2 cup dry, white wine

4 tomatoes

1 teacup of rice

Salt, pepper

Wash the birds, salt and pepper them. Sauté in butter and then add wine. Sieve tomatoes and add to pot. Then add 2-1/2 teacups of water and the rice. Allow to cook all together for 25-30 minutes over low heat.

● **Duck with peas** ● **Turtle-doves with rice** ● **Hare with prunes**

Hare with prunes (from Macedonia)

[Lagos me damaskina (Macedonias)]

6 servings

1 hare (1-1/2 kg)
250 gr prunes
250 gr bacon
250 gr onions
4 tbsps corn flour
8 tbsps butter
Salt, pepper

Marinade

1 bottle red wine
2 carrots, peeled
2 onions, peeled
3 cloves garlic
2 bayleaves, thyme
Sage
2 tbsps vinegar

Clean and wash hare, cut into servings and place in a large bowl. Slice carrots, onions and garlic and place in bowl with the hare. Add wine, vinegar, bayleaves, thyme and sage. Leave to marinate overnight. The next day, salt and pepper the hare and sauté it in butter. Cut the bacon into small pieces, add it to the pot with the hare, fry for a few minutes and then add the marinade, onions and prunes. Cover the pot. Cook over low heat for about one hour.

Wild duck (from Naoussa)

(Agriopapia Naoussas)

2 servings

1 wild duck
1 sour apple
Salt, pepper, a little thyme
3 tbsps butter
A little oil
1 carrot
1 onion
1 clove
1 bayleaf, parsley
1 hot pepper
1 garlic clove

Clean and wash the wild duck. Peel and slice apple thinly; add salt, pepper, thyme and parsley; stuff the duck with this mixture. Place in small buttered roasting pan, rub with oil, cover with foil and bake in moderate oven for 30 minutes. Peel and chop onion, carrot, garlic and pepper. Place butter in a frying pan and sauté the onion, carrot, garlic, pepper, bayleaf and clove. Add salt and pepper and a little water and simmer for a few minutes. Remove foil from duck, pour over this sauce and replace foil. Let it bake for about another hour. When bird is tender, cut into servings and garnish with sauce.

Roast stuffed wild duck (Agriopapia yemisti)

4 servings

1 wild duck

1 kg mushrooms, sliced

3 onions

Finely chopped parsley

Thyme, salt, pepper

4 tbsps vinegar

4 tbsps butter

Fill a pot half full of water. When the water comes to a boil, put duck in and boil for 10 minutes. Peel and slice onions. Put oil and butter into a frying pan with the onions and mushrooms and sauté for a few minutes. Add the parsley, thyme, salt and pepper and stuff the duck with this mixture. Sew up cavity. Place in buttered pan and bake in preheated moderate oven for 40 minutes or until duck is tender. Serve on a platter garnished with the stuffing.

Wild boar with olives (Agriogourouno me elies)

6 servings

1-1/2 kg wild boar

1 teacup oil

1 large onion, shopped

1 cup red wine

1 tsp tomato paste

250 gr black olives

Salt, pepper

Cut boar into 6 portions. Heat oil in pot and sauté the meat. Sauté the onion and then add the wine, salt, pepper and tomato paste diluted in water; cover the meat with water and allow to boil on a low heat for about one hour or until tender. Just before removing from heat, add the olives and cook for 15 minutes more. Serve the wild boar on a platter; pour over the sauce.

Salmi of wild boar (Agriogourouno Salmi)

7-8 servings

2 kg wild boar

3 cups red wine

1 carrot

1 cup of brandy

1 stick of celery

Salt, pepper

2 onions

1 bayleaf

Rosemary and thyme

1/2 cup butter

4 peeled tomatoes

Cut meat into 8 servings and place in a bowl. Peel and slice onions and carrot. Chop celery. Place vegetables in bowl with meat, along with thyme, rosemary, wine and brandy. Cover and allow to marinate for 24 hours in the refrigerator. Strain marinade. In a large pan, sauté meat in the butter. Sieve tomatoes and add to the meat together with the marinade and all the vegetables. Cook until meat is done. Remove meat from pan and boil the sauce until thick. Sieve it and pour over the meat. Serve with fried potatoes. All game, hare, wild duck, etc. can be cooked in the same way.

sweets

Sweet Easter bread (Tsoureki)

2 kg all purpose or durum flour

200 gr fresh yeast

1 teacup warm water

3 cups sugar

1 tsp salt

2 tbsps oil

1 tsp mahlepi (ground)

1 tsp mastic from Chios (ground)

1 teacup warm milk

1-1/2 teacup butter

10 eggs

In a large bowl, put the yeast in warm water for about 10 minutes and cover. Then add enough flour to make a thick batter and stir. Cover and leave for about 30 minutes to double in bulk. In another bowl, place the sugar, flavourings, salt and oil. Add the warm milk and blend well. Beat the eggs and add to batter, mixing lightly with the hands. Add the yeast and mix well. Then add the remaining flour and knead well. Add melted butter gradually, kneading well until the butter is all used up. The dough is now warm and soft. Place in a bowl, cover with a blanket for 1-2 hours or until doubled in bulk. Do not knead the dough again, but divide into 21 pieces. On a floured board, shape ropes about 12 inches long and 3/4 to 1 inch in diameter. Plait braids using three ropes at a time. Place on an oiled baking sheet, cover with towel and allow to rise for 30 minutes. Brush with diluted egg yolk, sprinkle with blanched almonds and bake in hot oven for about 30 minutes.

(Note: mahlepi and mastic are characteristic flavourings in this type of sweet bread. You should be able to find them in a Greek grocery shop. If you can't find both, one will do just fine.)

Chocolate cake (Keik sokolatas)

2-1/2 teacups flour

1 teacup butter

3/4 teacup cocoa

2 teacups sugar

6 eggs

1 tsp vanilla

1 teacup milk

Glaze

1 teacup icing sugar

2 egg yolks

125 gr bakers' chocolate

2 tbsps brandy

1 tsp milk

2 tbsps fresh butter

Place the cake ingredients in a mixing bowl. Mix lightly and then beat with mixer for 4-5 minutes. The batter should be frothy. Pour into buttered cake tin and bake in moderate oven for about 1 hour. When it has cooled, turn out onto a platter. Meantime, prepare the glaze. Melt the chocolate in the top of a double boiler. Add remaining ingredients and mix well. Pour glaze over cake.

Kadaifi (Kadaifi)

1/2 kg kadaifi dough

1/2 kg coarsely chopped walnuts

1/4 teacup toast or rusk crumbs

1 tsp cinnamon

1/4 tsp ground cloves

1/4 teacup sugar

4 tbsps brandy

2 teacups butter

Syrup

3-1/2 teacups sugar

2 teacups water

1/2 teacup pistachios, coarsely
    chopped

I n a large bowl, mix together the walnuts, toast crumbs, flavourings, sugar and brandy. Divide the kadaifi into 30 long, thin strips. On the end of each strip place one spoonful of the filling and roll up gently. Put close together in a buttered baking pan. Melt the butter and pour over each one with a spoon. Cover with aluminium foil and bake in a moderate oven for 30 minutes. Remove the foil and cook for another 30 minutes, until golden. Boil all the ingredients for the syrup for 5 minutes and pour over the kadaifi as soon as it is taken from the oven. Leave for a few hours until the syrup is absorbed, and place on a platter. Garnish with pistachios.

Orange cake (Keik portokaliou)

2 teacups sugar

3-1/2 teacups flour

1 teacup butter

1 teacup orange juice

5 eggs

3 tsps grated orange rind

4 tbsps powdered sugar

B eat all the ingredients with a mixer, except for the powdered sugar, for 5 minutes at medium speed until the batter is thick and foamy. Pour the batter into a buttered cake tin and bake in a moderate oven for about an hour. Remove from oven and turn out on a platter. Sprinkle with powdered sugar.

Easter biscuits (Koulourakia paschalina)

150 gr melted butter

150 gr sugar

600 gr flour

1/2 cup milk

1 level tsp baking powder

1 tsp vanilla or grated orange rind

B eat the melted butter and sugar with a mixer for 5-10 minutes. Add the milk and orange rind and gradually add the flour mixed with baking power. The dough should be quite firm. Make the biscuits in various shapes and bake in a moderate oven until done.

Butter biscuits (Koulourakia voutirou)

1/2 teacup softened fresh butter

1/2 teacup sugar

1 egg yolk

2 tbsps milk

1 tsp grated orange rind or vanilla

essence

2 teacups self-raising flour

Beat butter with a mixer and add sugar gradually. Continue beating and add the egg yolk, milk, and grated orange rind or vanilla. Add flour, stirring initially with a wooden spoon, and then knead the dough lightly. Refrigerate for 1 hour. Then shape dough into small biscuits, brush with beaten egg and bake in moderate oven for 20 minutes.

New Year's cake (Vassilopita)

500 gr butter

500 gr sugar

1/2 kg milk

1-1/2 kg flour

50 gr yeast

Grated rind and juice of 1 orange

3 eggs

1 beaten egg for glaze

Place the flour in a bowl with the yeast, eggs, butter, sugar, milk, orange rind and juice and knead well. When dough is smooth, cover with towel and let rise in a warm place. When double in bulk, punch down. Butter a flat baking pan and spread the dough in it. Allow to rise again. Then brush with the beaten egg and sprinkle with broken almonds or sesame seeds. Bake in moderate oven for 50 or 60 minutes. If it becomes too brown, cover with aluminium foil.

Turnovers from Crete (Skaltsounia Kritis)

32-35 pieces

4-1/2 teacups flour

1/2 tsp salt

4 tbsps oil

Juice of 1 orange

600 gr cottage cheese or other

unsalted cheese

2 eggs

1/2 tsp cinnamon

2 tbsps sugar

1/4 tsp baking powder

Oil for frying

To make the dough, mix the flour, baking powder, oil and orange juice and knead. Set aside and cover with a towel for about an hour. Mix the cottage cheese with the eggs, sugar and cinnamon. Roll out dough to about the thickness of a coin. Cut into circles. Place a spoonful of the cheese mixture on each circle of pastry and fold over. Moisten edges and press down with a fork so the turnovers do not open. Fry. While still hot, sprinkle with icing sugar and cinnamon.

Kadaifi from Yannena (Kadaifi yanniotiko)

20-25 pieces

1 teacup coarsely chopped walnuts

1 tsp cinnamon

1/2 kg kadaifi

250 gr phyllo dough

1 teacup butter

Syrup

4 teacups sugar

Peel of one lemon

2-1/2 teacups water

1 cinnamon stick

Butter a baking pan and spread half the phyllo on the bottom, brushing each with butter. The phyllo should come up above the top of the pan. Spread half the kadaifi in the pan over the phyllo. Sprinkle the walnuts and cinnamon evenly over the kadaifi. Spread the remaining kadaifi over the walnuts. Fold over the bottom sheets of phyllo. Add the remaining phyllo, buttering each sheet. Pour over the rest of the butter. Score the top two layers of phyllo in squares with a sharp knife. Bake in moderate oven for about an hour. To make the syrup, boil the ingredients for a few minutes to bind and allow to cool slightly. Then pour over the kadaifi. Cover and allow to stand for about 30 minutes.

Milk pie from Macedonia

(Galaktopita Makedonias)

18-20 pieces

Dough

1-1/2 teacups flour

250 gr butter

1 pinch baking powder

Few grains salt

Water as needed.

Cream filling

10 level tbsps flour

1 teacup sugar

4 teacups milk

Grated rind of 1 orange or lemon

4 eggs

Icing sugar

1/2 tsp cinnamon

First prepare the dough as follows: Place flour, baking powder, butter and salt in a bowl and knead well. Set aside for about 1 hour. Prepare the cream filling. Beat eggs with sugar until light. Add the flour and 1 cup cold milk and mix well. Heat 3 cups milk. When hot (not boiling) add the egg mixture, stirring constantly. When filling thickens remove from heat and add the grated orange rind. Divide the dough in two. Roll out dough and place one sheet in a small, buttered baking pan. Pour in cream filling and cover with second sheet of dough. Score the top of pastry lightly and bake in moderately hot oven for about 45 minutes. When cooked, sprinkle with icing sugar and cinnamon.

Baklava (Baklavas)

1/2 kg phyllo dough

2 teacups coarsely chopped
  almonds

2 teacups coarsely chopped
  walnuts

1 tsp cinnamon

1/4 tsp cloves (ground)

Cloves (whole)

1 teacup butter

Syrup

3 teacups sugar

2 teacups water

1/2 teacup honey

2 tbsps lemon juice

2 tsps vanilla

In a bowl, mix the walnuts, almonds, cinnamon and cloves. Melt butter, butter a baking pan and put in four sheets of dough, buttering each one and making sure the dough comes up over the side of the pan. Sprinkle on some of the walnut filling and continue putting in buttered sheets two by two with filling in between until the phyllo dough is used up. Finish with 4 sheets of dough, as you began. Score the top of the pastry with a sharp knife in squares and put a whole clove in the middle of each. Pour over the remaining butter and bake in a moderate oven for at least 1 hour or until well browned. Cool. Boil the sugar, water and honey for 5 minutes. Remove from heat and add lemon juice. Pour hot syrup over the baklava. Allow to absorb the syrup and cool.

15 pieces

1-1/2 litres milk

100 gr fine semolina

300 gr phyllo dough

4 eggs

1 teacup melted butter

1 teacup sugar

Syrup

2 teacups sugar

1 teacup water

Peel of one lemon

Custard pie (Galaktoboureko)

Prepare the cream filling as follows: Heat milk with one teacup sugar. Add semolina gradually, stirring constantly until thick. Remove from heat. Beat eggs well and add to cream filling. Butter a large baking pan and spread over half the phyllo dough, brushing each sheet with melted butter. The phyllo should come up above the top of the pan. Pour in the filling and fold over the bottom phyllo sheets. Cover with the remaining sheets, buttering each one. Pour over remaining butter. Score top two sheets, and bake in moderate oven for about 1 hour. Allow to cool. To make the syrup, boil 2 teacups sugar, 1 teacup water and the lemon peel in a saucepan for 5 minutes and pour over the pie.

● Baklava ● Custard pie

Honey puffs (Loukoumathes)

3-1/2 cups flour

1 cup warm water

1 cup warm milk

60 gr yeast

1 tbsps sugar

1/2 tsp salt

4 tbsps oil

Oil for frying

Honey, cinnamon

Put yeast in warm water in a large bowl and cover for 10 minutes. Add the flour, milk, sugar, salt and 4 tbsps oil to the bowl and beat with mixer for 2-3 minutes at high speed until smooth. Cover the bowl and leave in a warm place to rise. Put enough oil for frying into a saucepan and heat until it begins to smoke. Dip a spoon into water, take a little batter and drop into the very hot oil. While the puffs are cooking, hold them down with a slotted spoon so they brown on all sides. Repeat until all the batter is used up. When fried, place on a platter and pour over the honey and cinnamon. Serve hot.

Apple pie (Milopita)

20-25 pieces

1 kg flour

500 gr butter

300 gr sugar

1/2 tsp baking powder

1 kg apples

1/2 cup sultanas

1 tsp cinnamon

1 tbsp butter

Place flour in a bowl with butter, sugar and baking powder and knead. If necessary add a little water to make a smooth, soft dough. Peel and slice apples into a buttered pan. Divide dough in two pieces, one a little larger than the other. Roll out the larger piece of dough and place in a 9X13 inch buttered baking pan. Add the apples, cinnamon, raisins and 1/2 cup sugar. Roll out second sheet of pastry and cover apples. Score top of pastry into squares. Bake in moderate oven for about 1 hour. If top browns too quickly, cover with brown paper.

Country-style halva (Halvas horiatikos)

2 teacups butter

1 teacup almonds, blanched,

chopped and toasted

4 teacups sugar

5 cups water

2 tsps cinnamon

1/2 kg coarse semolina

Put the butter in a saucepan with the semolina. Stir constantly until semolina is browned. Then add the sugar, water and almonds. Continue stirring until the halva starts to thicken. Remove saucepan from heat, put mixture into a mould or tube pan for five minutes and cover with a clean cloth. Turn out onto a plate and sprinkle with the cinnamon. Cut when cool.

• Apple pie • Country-style halva • Walnut cake

Walnut cake (Karythopita)

16-20 pieces

250 gr butter

1 teacup sugar

3 eggs

Dash of cinnamon

1-1/2 teacup finely chopped

    walnuts

1/2 teacup milk

2-1/2 teacups flour

1 tsp baking powder

Syrup

2-1/2 teacup sugar

1-1/2 teacup water

1 cinnamon stick

C ream butter and sugar, add eggs one by one beating between each, and then the cinnamon and walnuts. Mix baking powder with flour and add to batter alternately with the milk. Butter and flour a baking pan or tube pan and pour in batter. Bake in moderate oven for about an hour. When done, boil sugar with water until syrup "binds" and then pour over the cake. Cool before cutting. Sprinkle with coarsely chopped walnuts.

Yoghurt cake (Yaourtopita)

20-24 pieces

3 teacups flour

1-1/2 tsp baking powder

1 teacup butter

1 tsp vanilla

1 teacup sugar

4 eggs

1 teacup plain yoghurt

1/2 teacup coarsely chopped,

    blanched almonds

Syrup

2 teacups sugar

1 teacup water

C ream the butter and sugar and beat with mixer for about 10 minutes. Add egg yolks. Continue beating. Mix baking powder with flour and add to batter alternately with the yoghurt. Beat with mixer. Beat the egg whites into a stiff meringue and fold into the batter. Butter a baking pan, pour in the batter and then sprinkle with the almonds. Bake for 90 minutes or until done. Boil the syrup until it "binds". As soon as the cake is cooked, pour over syrup. Cool before cutting.

18-20 pieces

2 teacups flour

3 level tsp. baking powder

1 teacup semolina

5 eggs

1 teacup sugar

1 teacup butter

1 teacup milk

1 teacup blanched almonds

Syrup

2-½ teacups sugar

1-½ teacups water

Juice of ½ lemon, Icing sugar,
   cinnamon

Semolina cake (Ravani)

Mix the flour, semolina and baking powder. Cream butter and sugar and add egg yolks. Add the flour mixture, milk and chopped almonds. Beat egg whites until stiff, and fold into batter. Pour into buttered baking pan and bake in moderate oven for 45 minutes, or until cake pulls away from the side of the pan. Boil 2-½ teacups sugar with 1-½ teacups water and the lemon juice for 5 minutes and pour the syrup over cake after cake cools slightly. Finally, sprinkle with a little icing sugar and cinnamon.

36 pieces

Oil for frying

1 teacup water

½ teacup butter

1 scant teacup flour

5 eggs

Syrup

1 glass sugar

1 glass honey

1 glass water

Doughnuts (Svinghi)

Put the water and butter in a saucepan. When it has come to a boil, drop in all the flour and stir constantly with a wooden spoon until mixed. Remove pan from heat and add one egg at a time, stirring batter constantly until smooth. Boil syrup ingredients for five minutes. Heat oil. Drop dough from a teaspoon into the hot oil. Do not put too many in at once. When the doughnuts are puffy and golden brown, remove with slotted spoon and pour over syrup.

30-32 pieces

1 cup unsalted butter

2-½ cups flour

1 teacup almonds, blanched,
   chopped and toasted

500 gr. icing sugar

1 tsp. rosewater

1 egg yolk

1/4 tsp. baking powder

Almond shortbread from Lamia (Kourabiethes Lamias)

Cream butter well with mixer. Add ½ cup sugar and the egg yolk and beat for 10 minutes. Add the rosewater, chopped almonds, flour and baking powder and knead well. Take a piece of dough about the size of an egg and shape into a crescent. Bake on lightly buttered baking sheets in a moderate oven for about 20 minutes. When baked, roll in icing sugar. When cool, sift icing sugar over them so they are well coated.

About 32 pieces

½ kg unsalted butter

1 teacup sugar

1/4 teacup brandy

7 teacups pastry flour

Icing sugar

Shortbread from Smyrna (Kourabiethes Smyrnis)

Beat butter and sugar well with a mixer. Add the brandy and flour and knead. Take pieces of dough about the size of an egg and shape into crescents. Bake in moderate oven for about 20 minutes. As soon as shortbeads come from the oven, roll in icing sugar. When they cool, sift over icing sugar so they are well coated. Arrange on platter.

½ kg. Self-raising flour

6 eggs

1-½ teacup water

3 teacups honey

2 teacups finely chopped walnuts

Oil for frying

Sweet fried bowknots (Thiples)

Beat the eggs and add the flour gradually to make a stiff dough. Divide the dough into 9 pieces and let stand for about 1 hour. Then roll out the dough as thinly as possible. Flour the dough frequently so that it does not stick. Cut the sheets of dough into thin strips (about 1 inch wide and 5 inches long) and pinch in the middle to make bows. Deep fry until golden brown. Remove from oil and place on absorbent paper to drain. Prepare the syrup by boiling the honey and water, and pour over thiples. Sprinkle with walnuts and cinnamon.

½ teacup olive oil

½ teacup butter

2 tsp. Sugar

Grated rind of 1 orange

1 level tsp. Cinnamon

1/4 tsp. Each grated nutmeg
   and cloves

4 teacups self-raising flour

½ teacup milk

Finely chopped walnuts
   and cinnamon

Syrup

1 teacup honey

1-½ teacups sugar

1 teacup water

Honey cakes (melomakarona)

Beat the oil, butter, sugar, orange rind and spices with mixer. Add 3-½ teacups flour and knead the dough. Sprinkle with the milk. Knead lightly with the remaining flour. Take a piece of dough the size of an egg and shape into an oval. Place cakes on oiled baking sheet. Bake in moderate oven for 30 minutes. Boil together the honey, sugar and water for three minutes. Skim off the foam and put in the melomakarona 5 or 6 at a time for a few minutes before they cool. Remove from syrup and arrange on platter. Sprinkle each one with walnuts and cinnamon.

• Sweet fried bow-knots • Shortbread • Honey cakes